Webtouch Selling

A high-touch sales model using the core online meeting software tools...an insider's guide to success

T. B. Hodge

www.webtouchselling.com

ISBN: 0985249919
ISBN-13: 978-0-9852499-1-5

DEDICATION

Webtouch Selling is dedicated to my loving and patient wife, Virginia, and my wonderful children Autumn and Lachlan. In many, many ways you all have provided me with the motivation to put my passion on paper. Thank you.

Acknowledgements

This book is being written for anyone, and everyone in sales. The goal is to help you and your organization excel in a world which demands newer, and more unique ways of staying in front of your prospects and customers. While I could thank the hundreds of people in my own organization who "pitch in" to the ideas, processes, and tribal knowledge you will find in this book, special thanks is warranted for several individuals.

First, thank you Alan Himmelreich for being at a random Walmart at the same time I was. Bumping into you as you were leaving and I was entering can only be associated with fate. We reminisced about our prior days at the investment firm where you were my manager, and spoke about our current careers. As you were telling me about your involvement in selling webtouch selling software, a light appeared to go off in your head, and you convinced me I would be perfect for the job. Now here I am, over four years later, working with you again, and enjoying all of the benefits of consulting with companies on implementing these same webtouch selling tools.

Thanks also to Brogan Taylor, our Regional Director at the time of my hiring. You must have seen that what I lacked in business-to-business sales I made up for in determination and motivation to succeed, a passion for selling, and an excitement about the product. Your knowledge and desire to escalate our successes will always be remembered. Thanks Brogan, you gave the final word on me being here!

Jeff, Gregg, Brian, Doug, and Steve...we all went through training together at about the same time, bounced thoughts and ideas off each other, and have all become great friends, as well as top tier Account Managers. Thanks for the willingness to discuss your tremendous ideas, secrets of success, and healthy competition.

To Chris Connelly, our current fearless leader...thank you for keeping the atmosphere one in which everyone feeds off of each other, facilitates an atmosphere of worthiness to the cause, and solidifies our continuous development.

Final thanks goes out to the numerous employees of my current employer for all maintaining a passion for webtouch selling, a desire to succeed, and motivations to make everyone around you excel at what they do.

Introduction

In early 2008, I began my current career as an Enterprise Software Sales Representative. Prior to my current role, I was doing inside sales for one of the largest investment companies in the world. Armed with a phone and email, I successfully reviewed hundreds, if not thousands of client investment portfolios. Now looking back, if I would have had the webtouch selling tools at my disposal, I would probably be retired and writing this book from my beachside lounge chair! In fact, as soon as I completed my product training at my current company, I tried my hardest to gain permission to call into my old employer as I knew webtouch selling software would be a perfect fit for their environment. Unfortunately, as you can imagine, that company was way out of my grasp. As the new guy on the block I was limited to companies with under 100 employees...they had over 50k.

$ *Word has it that this company just joined the webtouch selling world in a BIG way!*

Since joining my current employer, which is by far the largest provider of webtouch selling software, I have seen my sales skills, and my wallet, take on a new form (both for the better). I truly enjoy selling using the webtouch model, and helping organizations see successes through their own implementation. In an attempt to "broaden my territory", I decided to write this book and pass along all of my gained tribal knowledge to businesses and organizations around the globe. If you are in sales, you HAVE to read this book!

It must be noted that I have made every attempt to be unbiased in my writing, even though I am of course convinced that my company's webtouch selling software is the best (isn't every salesperson convinced their product is the best?!) But this book will NOT be a product push, and instead focus on the fundamentals of what webtouch selling is, how it will benefit your company or organization, how to use the tools, and how to go about choosing the right software provider. In fact, the book will be filled with insider information, best practices, and ultimately lead to secrets you should know about making this important move to a webtouch selling model.

This book is written for YOU...the person involved in any step of your organization's sales process. I was cautioned about indicating such a broad audience in this introduction, but praised after being read by some much respected peers. But let me explain a bit more what I truly mean by this statement:

- C-Level Executives, Presidents and Vice Presidents, Directors, and Managers - You will find value in the beginning chapters of this book by developing an understanding of what a webtouch selling model is, and whether it is a sales model worth implementing. The closing chapters will also provide you with valuable insight into the inner workings of the webtouch selling software providers and help you navigate the path to a successful purchase and vendor relationship.
- Sales, Marketing, and Support Representatives - The middle chapters of the book will focus deeply on how to effectively use the software both prior to and after purchasing. Additionally, these chapters will continue to serve as a reference guide for how-to's, best practices, and soft-skills which can be used to train new users and keep your sales team finely-tuned.
- IT - While not traditionally considered key members of a sales team, your importance is being more and more recognized. Reading the entire book will help you gain more perspective on the importance of how technology can help lead your

organization to a better bottom-line. And because most software purchases will filter through your group anyway, portions of this book will cover some technical aspects which technology departments typically deem important.

Evidence shows that virtualizing a sales team by using the webtouch selling tools will lead your production immediately on an upward trend. This book lays it all out, and will ensure that you understand what you are getting into, and where it will take you. Good selling!

Part I Foundations

Chapter 1 Getting Started

So let's cover what on earth we will be talking about, and why the heck you should spend your time reading this book! Ultimately it will boil down to increased sales numbers, and more money in everyone's pockets. Webtouch selling is catching on in organizations at a feverish rate, and adopters are quickly separating themselves from their competition.

We are excited to present this information to you, and from an insider's perspective. The writer and contributors to this book have over 20 years combined experience not only selling webtouch selling software to organizations, but using the webtouch selling tools to do it! We are unarguably some of the most successful webtouch sales reps on the planet, and will be sharing our tribal knowledge throughout.

What is Webtouch Selling?

Quite simply, webtouch selling is using online meeting software to "virtualize" your sales team, and create a high-touch sales model. WebEx...GoToMeeting...LiveMeeting. You may have heard of these services, and have probably seen several commercials about them. In fact, the chances are high that you have even taken part in or attended an online meeting, webinar, or training already. The true power behind these tools lies in their effectiveness to help increase the lifeblood of any organization...revenue! The webtouch selling suite includes applications for marketing, direct selling, training, support, and instant messaging/presence. What is needed for a webtouch selling model? A computer, an Internet connection, a web browser, and a sales team...that's it!

One major vendor publishes the following statistics on their website:

- Over 1 Billion web meeting minutes used per MONTH
- Over 200,000 web meetings per DAY
- Over 10 Million meeting participants monthly
- 150+ countries with unique web meeting participants

These are BIG numbers and help indicate just how important these tools are in the selling environment of many organizations. So let's dig a little deeper.

A webtouch sales model is an established way of using web conferencing and online meeting tools to directly sell to prospects over the Internet. Benefits include increased production, immediate reductions in travel expenses, and keeping in front of your prospects throughout the sales cycle. Webtouch selling also includes ways to use the online meeting tools to quickly generate qualified leads, keep your sales team and channel partners up to speed on product development and new sales strategies, and of course support your customers and keep them buying from you.

Typically, a complete webtouch sales model will include five core tools, each designed for specific roles in the sales process. These tools include a webinar, or online event application, a general meeting and presentation tool, an online training and eLearning product, a customer support application, and an internal collaboration tool such as Enterprise Instant Messaging and presence tool. It is important to note here that any of these tools used on their own will definitely add a lot of value to your sales efforts, but a true webtouch sales model will effectively utilize all five. We will focus on each one of them separately, and constantly mention how they work in conjunction with the others.

Webtouch Selling is a Selling Model which Integrates with your Sales Process

It is important to note that webtouch selling is not a “sales process”. But it is a model in which to execute your organization’s sales process. Make sense? If you are in sales, you must have a sales process. If you don’t, then use the remainder of this book to help you develop your sales process around this selling model!

Sales processes come in many different shapes and sizes, and usually include steps such as qualification, proposal, and closing. So to build on this example, the webtouch selling software can help you qualify leads through webinars and presentations, share proposals via an online meeting, and close the deal by sharing the contract just before signing.

Who Should Read this Book?

The primary audience to benefit from this definitive guide will be Managers, Directors, Vice-Presidents, and Presidents of their respective departments (sales, marketing, training, support). Every part of this book will provide value in helping to decide why a webtouch selling model, and how a webtouch selling model. While Managers and Directors will typically need the knowledge gained here to help decide what is appropriate and applicable for their groups, the VP’s and above will want to understand how everything fits together as a whole within the organization. This also brings in another set beneficiary, which are the C-Level executives ultimately responsible for the highest levels of understanding, and final decision making.

But while written at a level which will maintain the attention of these upper tier knowledge workers, the end user will be kept in mind as well. This will be especially true in the sections which focus on practical use of the individual tools. In addition to providing guidance on how and what to click on, soft skills such as getting the appointment and keeping the prospect engaged will be deeply focused on as well. So while some of the step-by-step processes will keep everyone in a learning mode, you will also stay entertained with some examples of what NOT to do!

At the end of the day, businesses and organizations have looked, and always will be looking for newer, more effective ways of driving revenue and staying ahead of the competition. It should be evident that the web is here to stay, and will always be a medium in which to facilitate sales. As long as webtouch selling tools continue to be available, they will continue to be used. And as long as all of the above remains true, a definitive book on webtouch selling should always have a place on the office bookshelf.

A Bit More on the 5 Core Webtouch Selling Tools

While individual chapters in this book are solely dedicated to each of the webtouch selling tools, let's briefly look at what we will be covering. The five core webtouch selling applications are as follows:

- A webinar or online event tool
- A general online meeting and presentation tool
- An online training and eLearning application
- An online customer support solution
- An Enterprise Instant Messaging tool

Each of these tools will have their own branding, which makes it a bit easier to distinguish what you are looking for/at. For example, the online meeting tool from CISCO WebEx is called Meeting Center, and the tool from CITRIX is called GoToMeeting. For larger online webinars or events, CISCO appropriately names theirs Event Center, and CITRIX calls theirs GoTo Webinar. The tools for training and support are also appropriately named.

So you can see here, the tools are purposefully built for their role, and appropriately named for the users benefit. Remember, many of these tools can be implemented on their own, and fit right in a current sales process. But effectively using all of them all will truly lead you to a complete webtouch selling environment.

Can my Organization Benefit from Using Webtouch Selling Software?

Organizations are constantly trying to find better ways to more efficiently meet with prospects and convert them into customers. They are consistently asking themselves these questions:

- How can we increase sales while lowering associated costs?
- How can we reach more prospects and customers faster and more often than our competition?
- How can we generate more qualified leads while reducing the cost per lead?
- How can we more effectively train our sales team, as well as our channels, so that everyone has the most up-to-date product knowledge?

- How do we better support our customers so that they continue to buy from us?

Webtouch selling tools cover these core areas, and help businesses achieve their goals.

Webtouch selling tools are fully developed and have proven themselves to be essential for thousands of organizations. Businesses of all sizes are spending between $500 and $1,000,000+ annually on webtouch selling software. Most have implemented this selling model only within the last 5 or so years, and of course many organizations have yet to begin using any at all (but they will). Some numbers show more than 90% of the Fortune 1000 companies are using these tools in some sort of capacity, while also indicating over 50,000 small-mid size companies are doing the same thing.

My experiences selling webtouch technology for the last several years have shown me that these tools can find a good spot in just about ANY organization, regardless of size, industry, location, etc. From the one-man shop who needs to meet more effectively with prospects and customers to the 60,000 employee organization whose 10,000 Account Managers use the tools daily for the same reasons, these tools have proven themselves as perhaps the most valuable application in the sales toolkit.

No organization's sales process is perfect. And in any economic environment, new and unique ways of presenting your offerings are a must to set you apart from any competition.

Seeing Results Quickly

Positive results will be achieved very quickly after a successful implementation of the webtouch selling tools. Inside sales teams can see an immediate impact on their effectiveness as the software can typically "drop-in" to their existing environment, and seasoned Sales Executives have found webtouch as a new way in which to "be in front" of their prospects and customers and maintain the "high-touch" approach they are so used to. Gone are the days of "I'll send you some information and follow up with a phone call" and here are the new glorious days of "let's hop into a web meeting so I can SHOW you what I am talking about". Are you familiar with the term "If you mail you fail"? Well it now applies to email as well!

If you have already begun to implement webtouch selling, then you have already seen the enormous benefits as they pertain to your business. Using the Internet for lead generation through webinars and direct selling through web presentations has helped numerous companies see immediate results. These results come in the forms of more qualified leads at a much lower Cost Per lead (CPL), reduced sales cycles, increased prospect focus and attention, large reduction in travel related expenses, and a new customer experience which focuses on attention and effective communication. If you are not staying in front of your customers and prospects, someone else is.

Understanding Which Companies Provide the Best Webtouch Selling Software

Vendors can come and vendors do go, but when it comes to finding a webtouch selling solution which will truly help transform your business, ensuring that the vendor can also act as a true business partner will prove to be an important part of the decision making criteria. Over the last several years, there has been an emergence of literally hundreds of "web conferencing" providers, each touting themselves as having unique functionality or "sexiness". However, there are really only a few TRUE providers of an overall webtouch selling solution. These key players include CISCO's WebEx suite of applications, CITRIX's GoTo products, Microsoft's collaboration software (Lync), and ADOBE's Connect platform.

Each of the above company's offerings, while solid in their own right, are slightly different and offer some key advantages over the others. There is an entire chapter dedicated to helping you understand the vendor environment. While many of these tools can be purchased directly from the company, better deals may be had by purchasing through their partners, or even 3rd party service providers, or SP's. I will stop short of "guiding" you to a specific company or vendor, and instead make certain you know which bases to cover, how to truly uncover your needs, what questions to ask, and how to effectively negotiate a contract!

Part II – Navigating the Software

Chapter 2 The Administration and Scheduling Interface

Accessing the administration and scheduling area of your webtouch selling software suite is typically pretty straightforward. For example one of the main providers creates a URL, or website, which you will login to in order to access your services. Some providers will even customize the site to mirror your company's website in order to extend your branding, and really make your site look like an extension of your website. This part can be important as it is also brands your login site so that when your attendees are joining your meetings they will continue to see your company logo.

The website itself has two main functions in that it serves as your administration area, as well as a place in which you can access advanced scheduling functionality.

The Administration Area

When you receive your login credentials to your service and first login, you may be prompted to install some add-ins, or what one provider calls "Productivity Tools". These tools are usually very small downloads that allow integration with other software you may be using, such as Microsoft Outlook for your email. The Outlook plug-in in particular will allow you to schedule a web meeting directly from your Outlook calendar, and will also allow you to make slight changes to your meeting preferences such as adding a password, allowing attendees to login early, etc. As a sales rep, I typically use the webtouch presentation tool with the same settings every time, and schedule about 99% of my meetings through Outlook. We will get into advanced scheduling later in this section.

Screenshot of WebEx Outlook Integration

You can see that by installing the Productivity Tools, icons are added to Microsoft Outlook to allow the user to easily add an online session to their meeting.

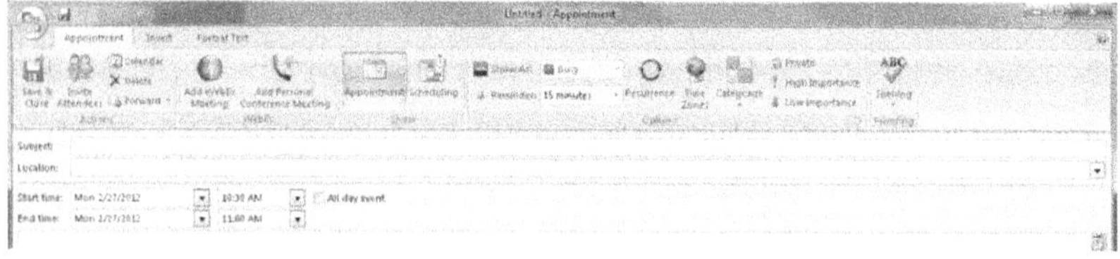

Once you are logged in as the administrator, you can perform several tasks. The main one will be to assign licenses to your users. For example, if you purchased multiple licenses for your sales team, you will want to create their own individual user accounts. Their accounts will usually be tied to their email address, and once their account is created, the system will automatically generate an email to them which will include their own personal login instructions. Once they have their login information, they will go to the same URL, login, and also be prompted to install the plug-ins.

Additionally, the administrator can make site wide changes and adjust individual user settings. These settings can include things like storage quotas, and access to only some of the webtouch selling software.

Administration Interface Screenshot

A user, or users, can be assigned administration privileges. When they click on the Administration link, they will be taken to a screen similar to this. As you can see, this simple interface makes it easy to control the user accounts, as well as some other “housekeeping” features.

ADVANCED SCHEDULING

As mentioned above, many users will schedule their meetings through their email program, or by using a 1-click option that sits on their desktop. But other times more advanced scheduling options will be needed. For example a certain meeting may require the attendees to be hidden, a separate conferencing bridge’s information to be used, or the meeting needs to be recurring. While some email programs allow these functionalities, not all do. So this area allows you to make these changes.

The other times this area will be accessed for meetings are when using some of the other webtouch selling tools. For example when scheduling a webinar, there are many things which you will want to customize such as email invitations, registration pages, and destination URL's. Or if a large training is being scheduled, you may want to create breakout sessions or tests. The advanced scheduling area must be used for these types of meetings.

Advanced Scheduler Screenshot

The Advanced Scheduling area is typically used for the webinar and training tool in the webtouch selling suite, as they usually require customizations of things like emails and registration pages.

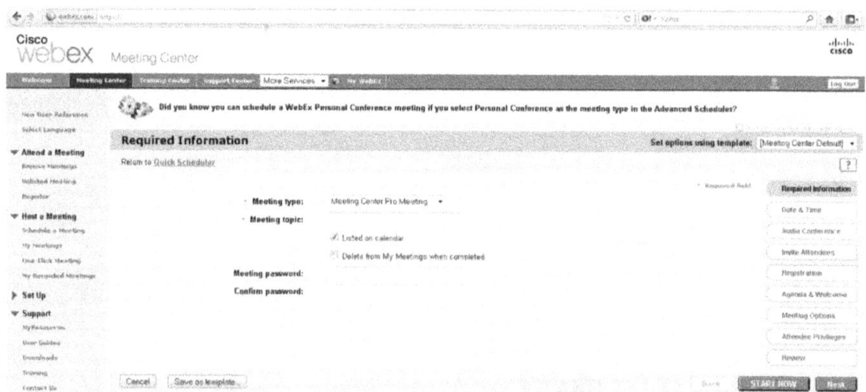

Other Reasons for Accessing the Administration Area

There are really none to speak of. The role you play in your organization's sales process, or which webtouch selling tools you are using will normally dictate how often and why you would need to login.

Chapter 3 The in-session Interface – participant panels

Now that you have an idea of what the interface looks like for setting up users, and scheduling meetings, let's understand what the software will look like when you are running a meeting, as well as what your attendees will see when they join.

Here are a few screenshots of the most popular software:

CISCO WebEx Screenshot

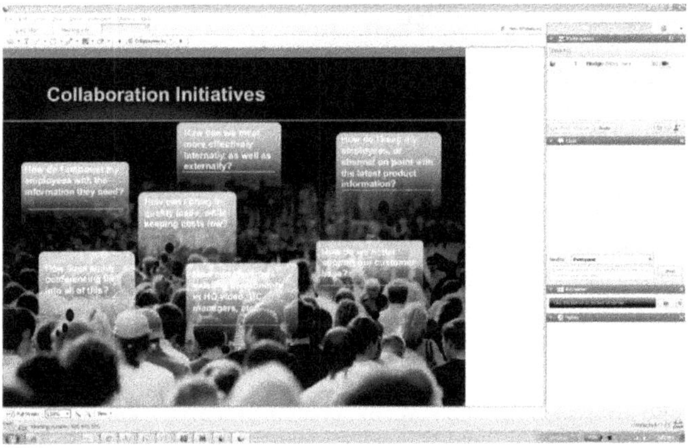

Microsoft Live Meeting Screenshot

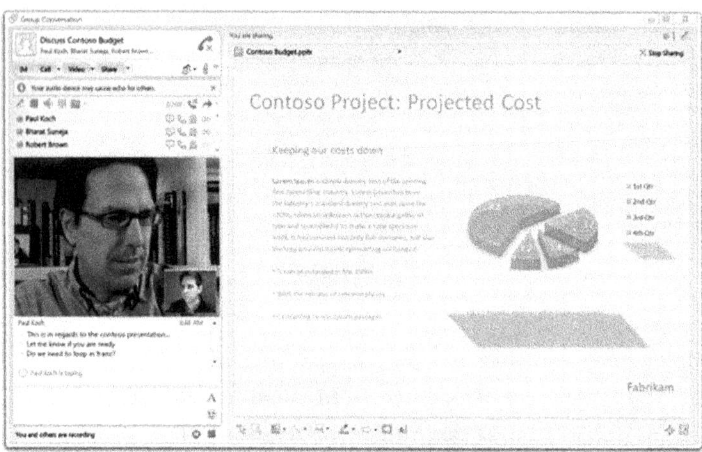

CITRIX GoToMeeting Screenshot

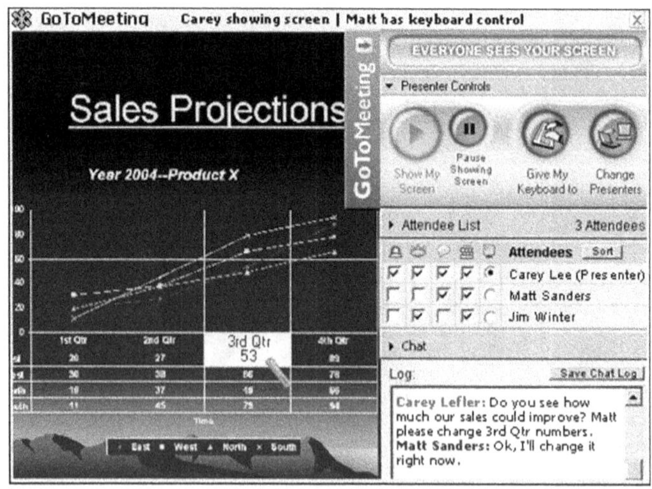

Adobe Connect Screenshot

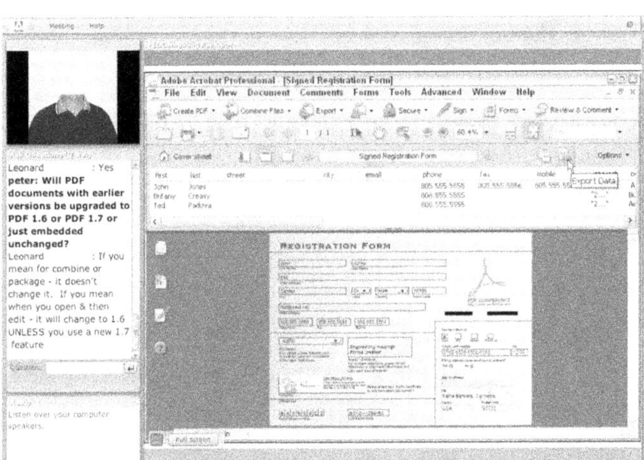

PANELS

When you login to your meeting, you will see two main areas. We will call one of the areas the "panels" area, and the other the "viewing" area. The panels area will typically have around eight different panels, which can be made visible, or hidden by the meeting organizer.

As you can see, the panels area is what you will access to control your meeting while it is in session. There are usually several different panels you can choose to have visible here, each providing specific functionality and control of your meeting. And don't worry about forgetting to add or take away panels during your advanced scheduling. If you need to make changes after the meeting has started, most software allows this to happen.

Let's take a look at the different panels you will typically find in your webtouch selling software. Please note that not all panels are found in each of the tools. Make sure that if you specifically need one of the panels that it is included in the webtouch selling tool you will be using.

Participant Panel

The participant panel will typically list who is actually in your meeting. When someone logs into your meeting, they are usually required to type in their name, email address, and sometimes other information. Their name will be populated into the participant panel so you can see who is in. While difficult for uninvited people to join one of your meetings, you still want to scroll through and make certain you recognize all of the participants. If you have an uninvited guest, you have every right to ask them who the heck they are. But be careful! Your prospect may have forwarded your invitation to someone else internally and you may not want to offend them.

Another purpose of the participant panel is to allow you to control the audio portion of your meeting. Your software should put some type of icon next to each attendee's name once they call in, or join via VoIP. This is another indicator that everyone has joined, and can now hear the conversation. Once everyone is connected to the audio portion, you should be able to mute and un-mute the group both as a whole, or individually. For example...we have all been in a conference where someone puts the group on hold, or joins from their convertible as it races down a highway. Your software should indicate where that noise is coming from through some type of "active talker" indicator, allowing you to mute that line individually. In other scenarios, where perhaps you have a large audience, it can help to mute the group as a whole, and then open up the audio lines for a Q & A session at the end.

The last real function of the participant panel is to allow control of who is doing the presenting. If there are multiple presenters in a meeting, training, or webinar, it is important for control to easily be passed when it is that person's turn to run the session. Some software allows you to simply drag and drop an icon to pass control of the meeting, while others allow you to right-click and assign the privilege. The process may be different with all of the webtouch selling software, but the concept is the same, and the functionality should be there.

A Participant Panel Screenshot

The participant panel shows you who is in the online session, and usually has a phone icon to indicate when they have joined the audio portion.

CHAT PANEL

The chat panel is exactly as advertised. It is an area in which participants can chat with other participants and presenters during your online presentation, training, or webinar. Chatting privileges can be assigned either during the scheduling process or on-the-fly in your session. For example, you may want to disallow attendees from being able to privately chat amongst themselves and make it so they can only chat with the Host, presenter, or panelist. Chatting functionality is usually used in smaller meetings, while Q & A is used in larger ones (see next section).

A Chat Panel Screenshot

The chat panel allows participants to chat publicly with the group, privately with other participants, or only with the Host or Presenter.

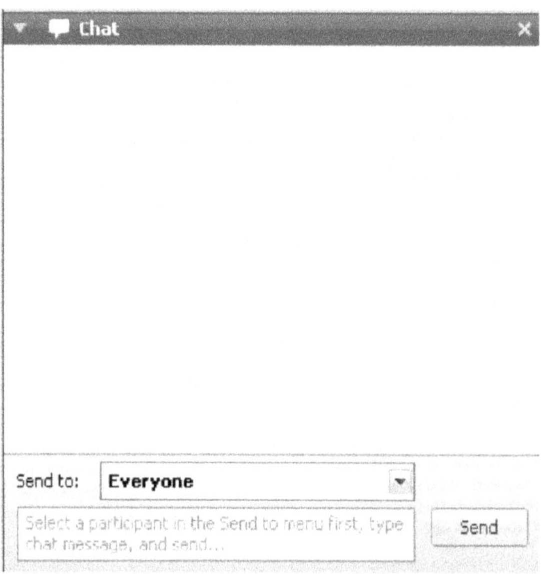

Q & A Panel

Similar to the chat panel, this is where attendees can type in questions. One of the key differences in Q & A versus chat however, is that the Q & A is much easier to manage. To compare, let's say there are 10 people in your online session. The chances are pretty high that more than one person will type in a chat at the same time. If multiple people are chatting in questions, then whomever is typing in the answers for the group to see will have a hard time indicating which question their answer pertains to! The Q & A panel is different, as it is considered "threaded". Threaded means that whomever is administering the Q & A panel simply needs to click on the question, type in the answer, and the answer appears directly beneath the question it pertains to. See the BIG difference? Q & A should also be able to be saved after the meeting is over in the form of a text file.

Q & A Panel Screenshot

The Q & A panel is similar to the chat panel, but allows for much easier management of questions from participants.

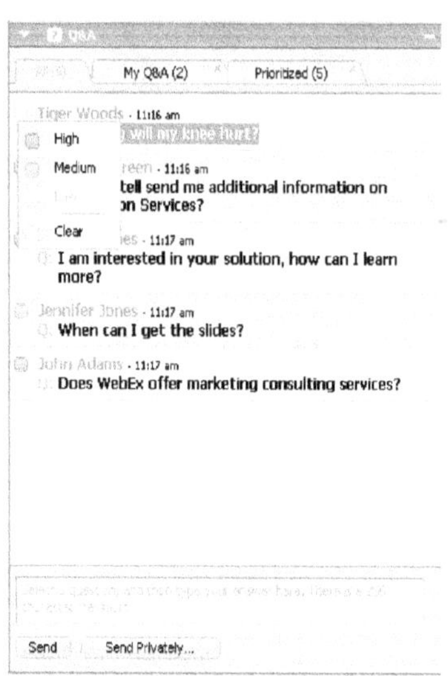

NOTES PANEL

Most webtouch selling software will have a panel available where attendees can type in notes during the meeting. This should be pretty straightforward, and also allow the attendee to save their notes once the session ends. Other online sessions may have a "note taker" assigned, and this will of course be the panel for them to use.

Notes Panel Screenshot

The notes panel can be used by participants to type in their own notes. It can also be used by someone assigned to take notes for the group.

Video Panel

The video panel is where attendees will see any webcams that may be broadcasting during the session. Usually the presenter will take up a larger part of this panel, while any other webcams will be shown below. This area should also include the icons for turning on and off the webcam, as well as making any needed adjustments for lighting, contrast, frames-per-second, bandwidth, and resolution. And while all of them will allow each user the control to turn their camera on or off, some of the more advanced webtouch selling tools will automatically make the other adjustments based on each user's connection speed. Ask about this...it can be important if your sessions will be using a lot of video.

Video Panel Screenshot

The video panel will show everyone who is broadcasting their webcam to the group. Different webtouch software will allow different amount of videos to be seen at one time.

POLLING PANEL

The polling panel is a popular panel used to gauge the attention of the group, and make the session a bit more interactive. Polls can usually be created prior to the session and easily be brought in on-the-fly. Additionally, polls can be created once in the session and after it has already started. Creating polls on the fly is commonly performed to grab the attention of your audience or gain their feedback on a recently discussed topic. After the group of attendees has been polled, the presenter can usually share the results with the group if desired.

Polling Panel Screenshot

Polls can usually be created prior to the session, and either pre-loaded or brought into the meeting on-the-fly. They can also be created ad-hoc, which can be helpful to gauge the attentiveness of your participants or test their retention of information.

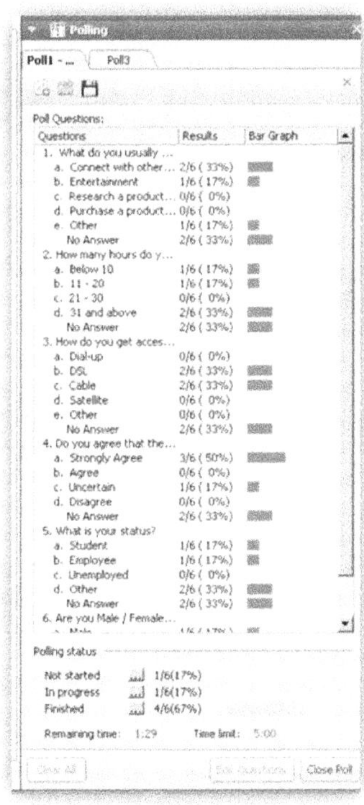

Recording Panel

This is a small panel, and will typically just have buttons to record the meeting, pause the recording, and stop the recording. Options will usually include the ability to record to your provider's servers, or record to your desktop. As these recordings can be large in size, choosing to record to your provider's servers, and have them host it for you is the usual method used.

Recording Panel Screenshot

Recordings can usually be started, paused, and stopped using he icons on this panel.

Media Viewing Panel

Some of the webtouch selling software has recently included a newer panel called the "media viewing panel". This area can be used to share media, such as a video or DVD. There is some extra work and hardware installation which needs to happen on the back end such as hooking up the DVD player to the computer, but once done this feature can be used quite effectively.

What Panels Do Your Attendees See?

For the most part, your attendees will see all of the panels that you have chosen to include in the session. For example, if you have decided that the Notes panel is just taking up space, and decide to remove it for the session, the attendees will not see it or have access to it. It is good to note here that your attendees will probably be able to manipulate them on their side. So even if you have included all of the panels, the attendee can toggle them so that they do not see them. However, if they have minimized the chat panel, and a chat comes in, they should see a blinking chat icon letting them know there is a new comment in the chat panel (applies to some of the other panels as well).

Summary

The panels area in your meeting is where all of the control takes place. The panels also allow users to interact with the hosts, presenters, and/or panelists and help facilitate the overall communications.

Remember to make certain that the webtouch selling tool you will be using has the appropriate panels for your specific online session.

Chapter 4 The in-session Interface – viewing area

While the panels area usually takes up a small percentage of the whole screen, say 20% or so, the viewing area takes up the rest. Quite simply, the viewing area is where your presentation will show up and be seen by the attendees. When everyone is settled in, and you pull up your presentation or file, it logically will take up the majority of the screen. Let's take a closer look at what happens in the viewing area.

Meeting Information

When attendees first join, the viewing area is usually blank, except for the general meeting information. Other than confirming for the attendee that they are in the correct meeting, this area can also indicate audio information for the attendee to access the dial-in bridge. Some providers also allow some customization of this area so that the presenter's names can be listed, or an agenda can be displayed. It is usually important to leave this meeting information visible until all of your attendees have joined. This will keep questions such as "How do I join the audio portion?" out of the chat area.

<u>Meeting Information Screen Screenshot</u>

This screen can help attendees know they are in the correct meeting. It also indicates the phone number of the audio bridge so they can join the audio portion of the session.

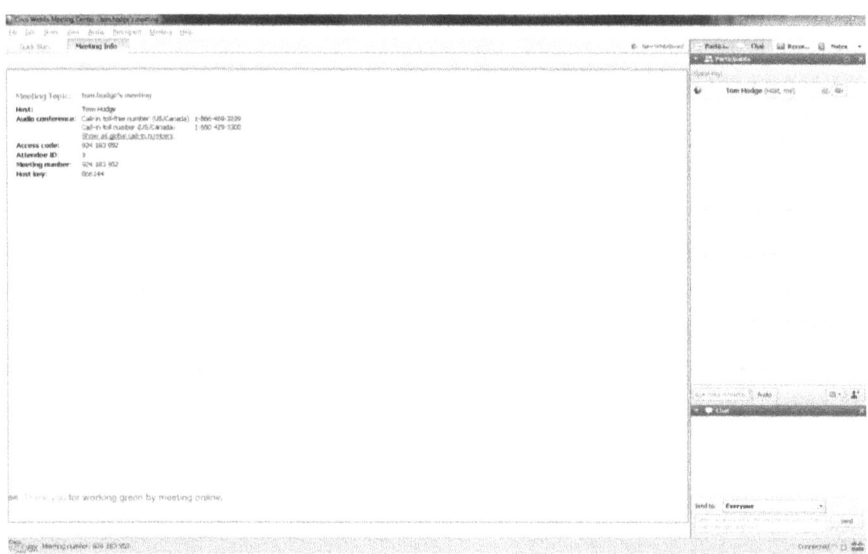

JOINING THE AUDIO PORTION

There are usually a few ways for participants to join the audio portion of your meetings. Perhaps the most common way is for them to call into a conferencing bridge via their office phone or cell phone. When there are several attendees joining from a conference room, they will usually dial in and put the phone on speaker. While typically the easiest and most common way to join the audio, it is also the most expensive as the "meter is running" on the audio minutes.

Another way to join the meeting is by VoIP. VoIP is becoming a more popular option as the cost is significantly less, and a lot of times free. The participant simply needs to be equipped with a VoIP headset, which plugs into their computer, or have a microphone and speakers. One thing that makes this option not so popular is that you are relying on your participants to have the setup to join this way, and feedback from microphones can be disruptive.

A third way an attendee can join the audio is by simply listening through their speakers. In this setup, the presenters will be the only ones calling in, and participants simply need to have speakers attached to their computers. This type of audio setup is typically used in webinars where attendees will not be speaking to the group. We will cover this more in that section.

Regardless of which way is chosen, the webtouch software will usually make it easy for the attendees to join. Below is a screenshot of a popup window attendees see when joining a meeting:

Sharing Content

Most of the webtouch selling software will make it as easy as possible for the presenter to share content. This is usually accomplished by putting a large icon in the middle of the viewing area that only the presenter can see. This icon usually says "SHARE"...easy huh?! Clicking on this icon will bring up options to share a file, application, web browser, whiteboard, or desktop. When "file or presentation" is chosen, a search window appears to the presenter. This window usually defaults to the "My Documents" folder, making it easy for the user to search for the document they want to share.

If you choose to share an application, you will typically see all of the applications currently running on your computer. This makes it easy to share one you have already opened prior to your online session. If you do need to share an application which you did not open prior to your meeting, you should be able to easily start and share it on the fly. Sharing your browser is the same as sharing an application, but will usually start you on a blank web page. From there you can take the attendees on a "tour" of a website by simply browsing.

Sharing your desktop is another option from this menu. When you choose to share your desktop, everyone's screens will probably flicker once or twice, and then everyone is viewing your desktop. Note that sharing applications, web browsers, and desktops usually takes place in full-screen mode automatically (more on this later).

Sharing Popup Screenshot

The sharing popup screen makes it easy to choose the content you want to share in your session.

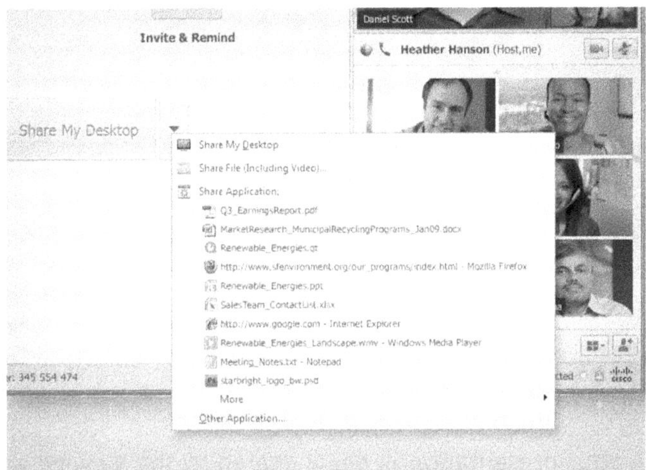

TABS

Most of the webtouch selling software will allow you to "pre-load" several different presentations into your session. This is used quite often when either multiple subjects will be covered, or multiple presenters will be presenting. When more than one presentation is loaded into the meeting, they will be separated by tabs towards the top of the viewing area. Whichever presenter currently has control of the meeting can click on whichever tab has their presentation. Additionally, these tabs can usually be renamed in the session. This helps different presenters easily find their presentation.

Tabs Screenshot

The tabs in this screenshot represent multiple presentations loaded into the meeting. Some of the webtouch selling software will allow you to rename the tabs, making it easy for multiple Presenters to quickly find their presentation.

FULL-SCREEN MODE

While your presentation is being shared in the viewing area, it will maintain the majority of your screen. Even if attendees minimize panels, the viewing dimensions stay the same. That is unless the presenter clicks on the full-screen icon. By doing this, the presenter sends the presentation to a full-screen view for everyone in the session. The panels area will usually be minimized automatically here, and show up as a "floating toolbar" somewhere on the edge of the computer screen. In addition to full-screen mode, most webtouch selling software will allow users to adjust the viewing in percentage terms...such as zooming in 115% for those with small screens, or joining from their cell phone. Note that even if the presenter sends the presentation to full-screen, the attendees will be able to go back to the normal view, and then back to full-screen on their own. Locking the full-screen view is a feature we have not yet seen in any of the webtouch selling software.

Other Purposes of the Viewing Area

Just as a shared file or presentation, the following will typically appear in the viewing area as well:

- Whiteboard
- Sharing web content
- Sharing pre-recorded videos

What is NOT typically seen in the Viewing Area

While files, presentations, whiteboards, etc are seen in the viewing area, other shared content is not. If you decide that you need to share an application with the group, this will usually happen in full-screen mode automatically. The same holds true for sharing a web browser, or desktop. But just as when sharing a file or presentation in full-screen mode, the panels are usually minimized to a "floating toolbar" near the edge of the computer screen. Again, when you do share an application, web browser, or desktop your screen will usually flicker once or twice, and the attendees will notice this as well. After the flicker, they will see what you are showing on your screen. A best practice before moving forward is to ask the group if they can now see what you are sharing. Some attendee's computers may take a tad longer than other's to catch up.

SUMMARY

The viewing area is the main area of the in-session interface that will display whatever is being shared. Maneuvering between regular and full-screen is a great way to grab your attendees attention, and help make sure they are focusing on your presentation, and not other areas of your session. Don't worry too much about remembering what shows up in the viewing area compared to what automatically displays in full screen as it will become evident to you as soon as you begin sharing your content.

Part III The Webtouch Selling Software Suite

Chapter 5 The Webinar Tool – Generating Qualified Leads

The lifeblood for any sales group is qualified leads. Sales reps rely on the marketing team to have a constant supply of leads which can be followed up with, and help build their pipeline. Unfortunately, there is no proven way to supply A-Leads 100% of the time. And even finely-tuned marketing campaigns will always welcome a little help. If you feel you have too many qualified leads to work with, skip to the section on "Converting Leads to Sales Using the Presentation Tool", and let me know if you're hiring! But if keeping your sales reps supplied with qualified leads and accurate contact information is an important initiative, read on.

Greenfield

Greenfield is a term used when targeting prospects, or non-current customers. As webinars are usually designed for large audiences and to "push" information to the group, marketers typically target prospects slightly differently than current customers. When planning your webinar, understanding what makes up a good prospect is vitally important. Your webtouch selling software should allow you to customize registration questions so you can derive the information about your prospects you are looking for. This is where the true power and features of your webinar application will pay dividends. It is one thing to be able to get hundreds of prospects into your webinar, but it is another to know exactly who they are, where they came from, and how qualified they are! Prospects aren't always forthcoming with information, so anything you can do "behind-the-scenes" will be a big help.

Current Customers

Of course webinars can also be done for your existing customers. These webinars can be scheduled to let your customer base know about new product releases, or enhancements to products they may already be using. The goals of these webinars will obviously be to create and recognize upsell opportunities. Some of the tracking and reporting features we are about to discuss will not necessarily be used, but the foundation will be set on how to plan those webinars as well. Additionally, a couple of the other webtouch selling tools we will discuss later in the book will show unique ways to keep your customers satisfied, close at hand, and hopefully wanting more!

Getting the Word out and Driving Attendance

You know you have a new product or service, and you know that time-to-market needs to be as fast as possible. Hopefully this is exactly why you have decided to have your webinar. So how are we going to get the word out and maximize attendance? We are going to use some of the most important features of the webinar software itself. Please take note here of how these options will fit into your existing marketing efforts, and offer many enhancements. Also make certain that these features are included with your solution. Again, it's one thing to have a platform which will support those 1,000 attendees you plan on having, but it is another thing to actually be able to get them to join!

CUSTOMIZED EMAIL INVITATIONS

Have you ever received an invitation to a webinar? Have you taken notice of the professional look and thought about how difficult it would be to do the same thing? Well it's not. In fact, the webinar tool itself will do much of the work for you.

Customizing your email invitations with a little HTML will add significant credibility to your webinar, and definitely draw the attention of potential attendees. Explore the "invitations" area in the scheduling section of your webinar software, and add pictures, color schemes, and other enhancements as you deem necessary.

Use the tracking functionality of the webinar tool. Your software should allow you to attach a unique value to the end of the registration link. This unique value will allow you to run your registration report and "track" which link was used to get the registrant to the registration page. This is an extremely useful feature which allows you to better understand several key pieces of information, including, but not limited to:

- Which email list had a better response rate
- Which list provider gave us the most valuable list for your money
- Which email had the best wording
- Which Google AdWords mixture gave you the best results
- Which rep had the best calling campaign
- What are your best affiliate sites
- Whether your mailers actually paid off

Many organizations begin their webinar initiatives and don't use these tools. This is obviously fine, as it is not imperative. However, once this functionality is effectively used they see their attendance increase, and their marketing efforts become more fine-tuned. Not to mention they save significant money by understanding where they are getting the most bang for their buck! Please see the "Real World Examples" at the end of this section for a detailed workflow.

Customized Emails

In this example, each of the email topics are links which can be clicked on. Clicking on the link will pull up a separate window allowing customization of that specific email.

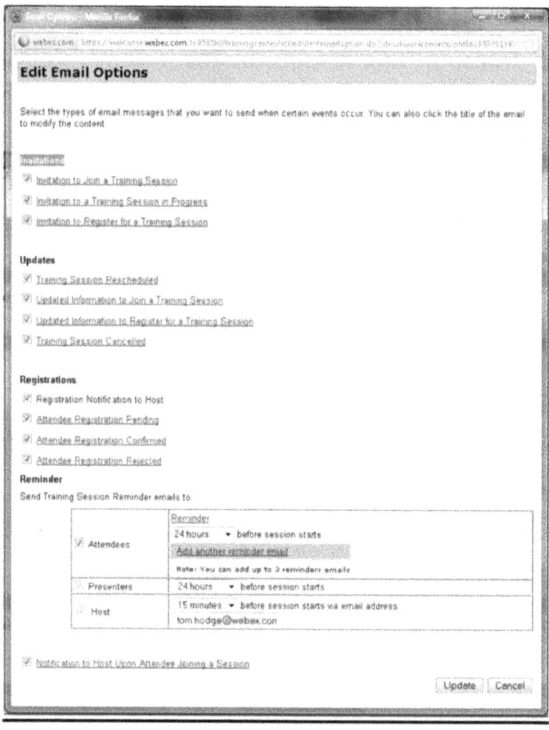

Customized Registration Page

Just as your email invitations can be customized with pictures, logos, color schemes, etc. so can, and should your event information and registration page. This registration page is where the prospect will be sent when they click on the link in their email to register for your event. Look at providing a professional picture of your presenter or Host, as well as some biographical information to let people know exactly who their presenter will be. An agenda should also be included here, along with any other information you want to provide.

This is also where you will configure your registration questions in an attempt to derive valuable information about the registrant. For example, besides the normal fields such as name, email address, phone number etc, you will also want to know more specific details which will help you "score" your leads. Did I just say "score" your leads? YES...score your leads! In the simplest way put, this means attaching a "weight" to their answers to your registration questions. In a very straightforward example, if I ask the question "When are you looking to make a purchase?", and they click on the option which says "Within 30 Days", I would weight this answer a 10. If they click on the option which says "We are at Least a Year Away", I would weight that answer a 1. Once you have done this with several of your registration questions, you will find that that registrant now has a value assigned to them, and therefore can be categorized as a good lead, a decent lead, or a bad.

Customized Registration Page Screenshot

Most webtouch software will give you pre-loaded choices of fields to add to your registration page. This provider also allows you to create custom fields for your registration page.

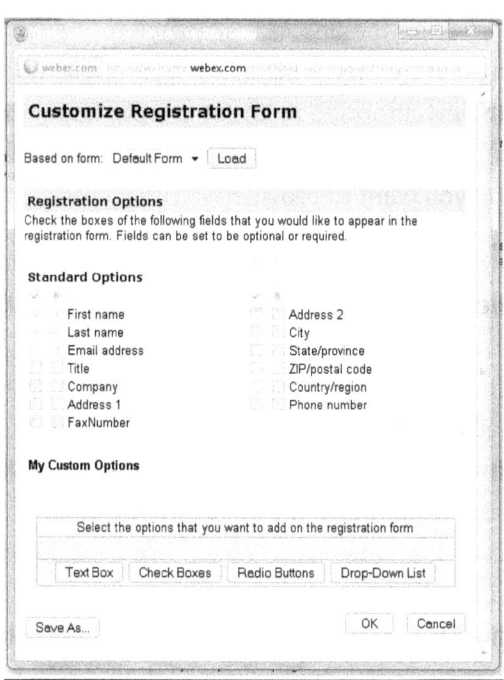

Reminder Emails

One of the biggest reasons that an organization's webinar lacks in the expected attendance is that the attendee has simply forgotten they registered, or they simply do not want to weed through hundreds of emails to find their login link and information. Your software should include the ability to automatically send out several reminder emails to your registrants, including one as close to the start time as you choose.

Don't Forget!!

Remember, you want to make it as easy as possible for your prospects to join. If they receive a reminder email the morning of the webinar, they are more likely to make any necessary adjustments to their day's schedule in order to attend.

Reminder Emails Screenshot

The below screenshot shows many options for scheduling emails. Additionally, this provider allows you to click on the underlined topics which will pull up a window allowing customization of these emails.

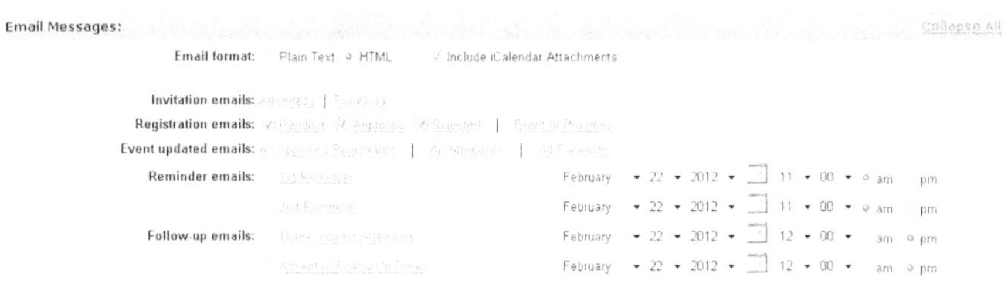

Email Messages: Collapse All

Email format: Plain Text HTML Include iCalendar Attachments

Invitation emails:

Registration emails:

Event updated emails:

Reminder emails: February 22 2012 11 00 am pm

February 22 2012 11 00 am pm

Follow-up emails: February 22 2012 12 00 am pm

February 22 2012 12 00 am pm

WHAT SHOULD YOU DO IN YOUR WEBINAR?

So the webinar is scheduled, the response rate is high, and everything is a go. Now what? Here are some examples of best practices and things to do with that hour your prospects have so graciously blocked off of their calendar.

Allowing Attendees to Join Before the Host or Presenter

If you are one that is constantly running late or just in case of an emergency, it is courteous to allow attendees to join the webinar early, and 15 minutes is usually a good rule of thumb. Experience shows that many folks like to join early in case they have issues logging in, or just want to get settled before the presentation. Do not overlook this simple setting as you would hate to lose prospects just because they could not join when they wanted to.

Mute Everyone Upon Entry!

Your webinar tool should have the option to do this. If it doesn't, look elsewhere! This is important in order to keep control of the group, and a courtesy to everyone in the webinar. Have you ever been in an online meeting or conference call and someone decides to put the group on hold? Or have you caught someone's side conversation going on because they forgot to mute themselves? This is all prevented when making sure that everyone's line is muted automatically. Some webinar software also includes the ability to simply "broadcast" the audio, in which only the presenters and panelists will actually be able to speak to the group, and all attendees will listen through their computer speakers. Please note this is usually the most cost-effective way of providing audio as well.

Using the File Menu to Mute Attendees

The "File" menu at the top gives the Host control of many different aspects of the meeting while it is in session. The "Participant" drop-down allows the muting and un-muting of the group, or individuals. Most webtouch software will also allow this functionality via an icon below the participants in the participant panel.

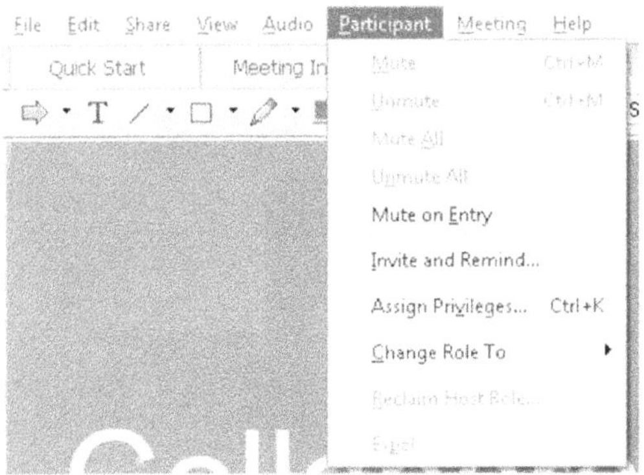

Hide Your Attendees

Only you need to know exactly how many people are actually in your webinar. Let me tell you...if you have a low turnout, say around 5 people and you were expecting 100+, your attendees will wonder what the heck they are doing there. So what can you do in this situation??? Act as if there are 500 attendees there and speak to the group accordingly! Thank them all for coming, let them know Q&A will be held until the end, and then seed in some questions. Sneaky? Maybe. A commonly used practice? Definitely. Additionally, this helps provide the privacy your attendees probably expect when joining a large group, which may include some of their competitors. And don't worry because you as the Host will always be able to see exactly who is in your webinar.

Loop a Pre-recorded Video, or Provide an Informational Slide

Organizations are more frequently using online meeting tools to present pre-recorded videos to prospects and customers. Not only does it get rid of the whitespace before your presentation, it keeps their attention and gets them ready for your message. Another best practice would include displaying an informational slide which may give direction on how to use Q & A, a list of panelists, timeline of presenters, or any other information you feel may be helpful to the group.

Remember that leaving the session and call-in information in the viewing area is also extremely important...maybe more important than looping information.

Make Your Introductions to the Group and USE VIDEO!

Introductions to your audience are an obvious component of your presentation. Use this time to let people know in your own words what will be covered, who will be presenting, and of course thank them for their time. And if you really want to leave an impact, flip on your webcam for a lasting effect! You don't have to leave it on the whole time, but letting them see your smiling face will add integrity to your initiatives and goals of a successful response. Of course some presenters do have the desire to leave on the webcam, and if you feel it will not draw attention away from your presentation, it is fine as a best practice. Just please don't be that person that forgets it is on! If you do forget, and have a funny story to share, please let us know on our blog at www.webtouchselling.com...we will all appreciate it!

Making Your Presentation

The meat-and-potatoes of this hour will be spent taking your audience through you presentation in hopes of building interest and awareness. The typical things you will be sharing with your group will be a slide-deck, your website, or even your software. All of these things can be easily shared using the webinar tool, so feel comfortable sharing one, or even all in your event.

Use the Q & A Functionality (different than chat)

Make sure that your webinar tool offers the Q & A functionality, and not just chat. If it doesn't, then look elsewhere. Keep in mind the main difference is in that a chat area has no organization, and if multiple people chat at the same time, it is almost impossible to follow or manage. Imagine having over 50 people in your webinar and several folks all start chatting in questions. Even if you can type answers as fast as the questions come in, your attendees will have trouble reading them and paying attention to your presentation at the same time. The Q & A feature is what's called "threaded", which simply means that if multiple questions come in at the same time, you only need to click on the question, type in the answer, and it shows up directly beneath the pertaining question.

Additional functionality in some webinar applications gives you the ability to go to the File menu, and save the Q&A as a text file. This file can then be converted to a Word doc which can be emailed out to your attendees, or even an html file which can be posted on your website. Allowing attendees, and even folks who could not join, the ability to review the Q&A is a commonly used best practice.

Destination URL

The destination URL is pretty much exactly as it sounds. You can have attendees automatically forwarded to a website of your choosing after your webinar. This could be a page to buy your services, receive information, or even take a survey. While the webinar application will usually allow you to create a post-event survey, some organizations prefer to use a 3rd party for this, such as surveymonkey.com.

Destination URLs can also be used to forward attendees to a website where they can schedule a follow-up with one of your sales reps. There are companies out there that can link with your calendars, and provide this service. Run a search in a search engine and you will find them.

Example of Adding a Destination URL in the Webinar Scheduler

This provider allows you to click on the "Select survey" link, and customize a survey. This survey will popup automatically once the session has ended. Another option here is to input a Destination URL, which can be any website you want your attendees automatically sent to once the session has ended.

Post-event survey: Select survey
Do not display survey to attendees
Display survey in pop-up window
Display survey in main browser window (instead of destination URL)
Destination URL after event: http://

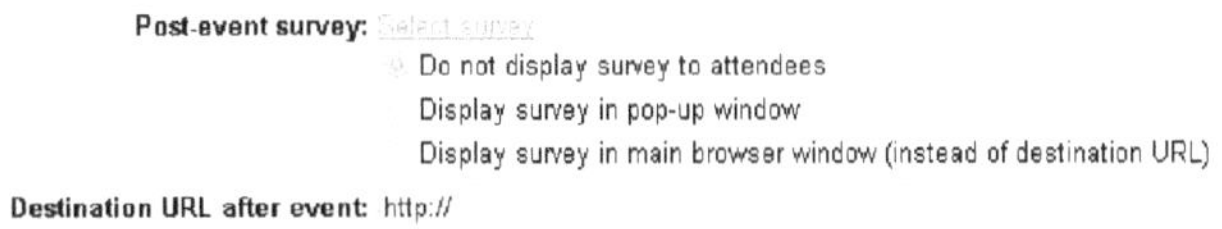

Recording Your Webinar

Make sure your provider gives you this functionality. One of the main vendors will actually host these recordings for you. This means that instead of having the file downloaded to your computer, they provide you a link. A link is much easier to work with than the large recording file (a 1-hour webinar usually equals about a 75MB file). This link can be posted on your website, and offers the ability to attach the same customized registration form which you used in your invitations and initial registration page.

While this hosted recording feature is used more often than not, the option to download it is also important. If you are recording a lot of webinars, you may run out of the included storage space your provider gives you. And even though additional storage is very inexpensive, you may want to download the webinars for backup purposes, compliance requirements, or other reasons. One of the top vendors not only allows both options, but they also make it very easy to convert your recording to commonly used file formats during the same download process.

Running Reports, and Finding the Most Qualified Leads from your Webinar

So this is where the fun starts, and begins the hunt for new customers. You just put in time and effort to make sure that you sent out effective email invitations, you setup your registration page to gather important information, and you pulled off a flawless presentation to what you feel should be new customers! What do you do now? You show your C-Level Executives that yes, marketing is an important area, and make it apparent that the sales folks need to buy you lunch and gift cards!

The administration area or control panel of your webinar software is where you will typically go to run your attendance reports. The data you will get from these reports will include much of the following:

- Complete registration information, including scoring of the registrant
- Information indicating if they actually joined, or registered but did not join
- Tracking statistics indicating where they arrived at your registration page from
- Attention statistics (some providers can actually track the percentage of time the viewer had your presentation at the forefront of their computer screen!)

This is definitely an area to explore as this data is ultimately your most valuable outcome from your webinars. Some providers can also provide you with Production Assistants who will help in the planning, presentation, recording, and post-reporting pieces of your event. Basically, they hold your hand the whole time. This can be money well spent if you are brand new to doing webinars and you would like some help in the beginning.

Example of Some Reports Which Can Be Run

Clicking on the links will take you to a screen where you can input parameters for your reports, and export in .csv, html, or .xls formats.

- Registration Report
  View registration information, and send reminder emails before the event. After the event, you can also view whether a registrant attended or was absent.
- Attendance Report
  View attendance information for any event. You can send follow-up emails after the event.
- In Event Activity Report
  View attendee activity information for an event.
  Note that the in-event activity report is only available for events recorded on the server.
- Attendee History Report
  View a list of events for an attendee.
- Event Recording Report
  View a list of attendees who have downloaded or viewed an event recording.

Real World Webinar Example

The Company

XYZ Trading is a company which educates individuals on investment trading strategies. They have a website which mainly sells some of their classes on DVD, as well as a book written by the founder. Additionally, they maintain online trading rooms which stay open during market hours and allow their paying members to login and look at real-time recommendations made by the meeting facilitator.

The Challenge

XYZ is the market leader for firms offering online trading rooms and technical advice. However, over the last couple of years there has been a tremendous amount of competition entering into the mix, which has reduced their install base, and resulted in a revenue drop. XYZ has introduced a new offering, which takes advantage of current market conditions, and communicating this new service offering as quickly as possible could help this revenue drop see an immediate turnaround.

The Solution

Simply adding this new offering to their website will not get them the results they are looking for. They understand the need to host a free webinar for prospects and customers, and want to gain the largest audience they can, while most importantly gaining qualified leads to follow-up on. XYZ currently has the following ways of getting the word out about their upcoming webinar:

- A list of email addresses for current customers

- A list of email addresses for past customers
- Three new lists of non-subscriber's email addresses purchased from three separate vendors

So now the Marketing Manager has access to their webinar software, and is logged in and creating the email invitations. There will be 5 separate emails sent out, one to each of their lists. Besides the main goal of gaining attendees to this webinar, it is also important to gauge the effectiveness and quality of the lists they have purchased. It has been decided that the wording in all of the email invitations will be the same, but knowing which list gets the best response is vital. Therefore, the software will be used to attach a unique code at the end of the registration link, which will indicate which email, and therefore list produced the attendee/lead. This information will be pulled from a report which is run through the administrative interface.

Additionally, they want to be able to distinguish good leads, bad leads, and some in-between. In order to do this, they will customize the registration page to include five questions, and require that they be answered (these are in addition to the obvious ones of Name, Email address, etc.). One of their questions is the following:

- How long have you been trading online?

The person registering will have 4 options, which range from 10+ years, down to less than 1 year. For XYZ, their ideal candidate is actually someone who has less time under their belt trading online, and therefore may be looking for an immediate way to become more knowledgeable. If someone clicks this option, they attach a score of "20" to that answer. However, they can also use the answers to the other questions to their advantage, and score them accordingly. The same registration report which is pulled to track where their leads came from will also attach a score to each individual registrant. This not only gives them insight into their audience, it allows them to organize the attendees into the most important leads to have their sales team follow up on!

Chapter 6 The Online Presentation Tool – Close More Sales!

Perhaps the easiest and most straightforward tool of the webtouch selling suite is the online presentation tool. This is the MUST HAVE in the Virtual Sales Specialist toolkit, and if used effectively will have an immediate impact on sales numbers. This application will generally have the least amount of features and functionality, but be most effective for direct sales presentations. For example, as most direct sales presentations are made to individuals, or small groups, the presentation tool will not do things like track where your leads are coming from (like the webinar tool does), and will not allow you to create breakout sessions for your attendees (like the online training application). So let's take a look at what it does do, and how it is used to sell.

Getting the Meeting - Inside Sales Teams

By now, you hopefully have a long list of qualified leads which were generated and handed to you on a silver platter by your marketing team through their effective webinars. We will make no such assumptions here, and instead simply focus on converting your leads, wherever they came from, including from cold-calling (ugh!).

If you are used to calling into a lead, hoping your timing is perfect, and then hoping you actually have their attention, you are in for a pleasant surprise. Or, if you are used to scheduling a call, having a good feeling about the conversation, but then are forced to email, or even snail-mail some information, you are in for an even more pleasant surprise. People are more than willing these days to take some time out of their day to listen to, and in this case view your sales presentation if they know it will be structured, and to the point. Letting them know it will be for no more than a set amount of time, usually an hour or so, and exactly what you will be covering makes getting them to agree to your meeting just that much easier. Additionally, knowing that they can join from the comfort of their own desk and that it will be delivered with some of the newest technology makes nailing down your appointment even easier.

So how do you get them to agree? There are a couple of proven ways to do this. First of course, call them and ask to compare calendars. Let them know that you want to invite them to an online meeting in which you will be discussing your product, and sharing content with them. Again, this could be in the form of a deck of informational slides, a tour of your website, a demonstration of your software, etc. If they agree, then use your webtouch software to send out the invitation immediately, and thank them in the subject line. Hopefully your webtouch tool integrates with your email program so you can access your calendar as you always would, and attach the meeting login credentials along with a link to click on and join. If not, then login to your webtouch software account, and schedule it that way. Your prospect will receive the link via email, and simply click on it to join your meeting.

But what if you cannot get through to them on the phone? Well it is not unheard of for a sales rep to simply email a meeting invitation to a prospect (a cold-invite). However, be prepared to include a nice email in the body explaining that you know they are busy, you have tried calling, and what the meeting will be about. If they accept your meeting, then congrats! You have found a new way of getting your foot in the door.

Getting the Meeting - Road Warriors

A lot of seasoned outside sales reps do not like to stray from the traditional way of nailing down an appointment...knocking on the door. Webtouch selling is not, and never will be an alternative to the outside rep making the house call. BUT, using the webtouch presentation tool to briefly show the prospect why they will be making their visit is starting to make a HUGE impact on the effectiveness of that visit. Additionally, the presentation tool is extremely valuable for follow-up until the contract is signed. Maintaining this high-touch process while staying off the road is catching on with even the most seasoned road warriors.

Several of the reasons above can also be applied to the prospect you will eventually see onsite. And gaining the appointment is typically done the same way. The difference will be evident later on in this chapter when we discussing getting contracts signed, and closing the sale. But for the outside sales rep, the webtouch presentation tool is used more for qualifying their lead before they hit the road. Once the prospect has seen the basics of what will be discussed, or even the entire presentation, the onsite meeting will have a more definitive purpose...either for further demo or presentation, or to put pen to paper.

Making your Presentation

So your prospect or group has joined your meeting, and it is time to begin. First, thank them all for their time and make sure everyone is still able to stay for the entirety. If someone needs to leave early, and you know they are an important beneficiary of a certain area of your presentation, you may need to make some last minute changes and cover the content intended for them sooner than planned. You do NOT want to find out later that the key decision maker left your meeting before you hit on a topic you knew would be important to them.

Next, even if you will be taking them on a tour of a website, or even giving a demo of a piece of software, you should present a slide which will lay out an agenda for the meeting. This will let them know that your meeting will be structured, what will be covered, and could perhaps get you some questions up front. Then ask the prospect whether or not they would like to add anything to the agenda. It is best to find this out up front, instead of them wondering the whole time and not paying full attention to what you are delivering. If they know that you have made note of it, and acknowledged that you will cover their concern or question in the meeting, then they are definitely more apt to pay closer attention to everything else.

So now it is go time. If you are making a presentation from a slide deck, you should already have it loaded into your meeting. This isn't the biggest of deals, as most webtouch solutions allow you to pull decks into the meeting ad-hoc. But having it pre-loaded can save time and show you are well prepared. You may need a presentation you thought you didn't, or may have accidentally loaded the wrong one. Not to worry, as loading a new one should take no time at all. If your software takes a long time to load your presentation, find another provider, fast. If you are going to be taking them on a tour through a website, then share your web browser. And if you will be sharing an application, then share that. It is all quite simple really. One thing to note though is the difference in desktop sharing, application sharing, browser sharing, and presentation sharing.

File Sharing

For those of you who will be working off of a slide deck, file sharing is the most common and best way to present. Sharing a file usually means you simply click on "share file" in your meeting. This will pull up a search box, which usually defaults to your "My Documents" folder. When sharing a file, it will typically pull up in the content viewing area of your web meeting.

Remember, the content viewing area takes up the majority of their viewing screen, and the panels are usually off to the side.

File sharing can accurately be compared to the transparencies many of us have seen either in school, or at on-site presentations before the days of laptops, projectors, and screens. When sharing a file, no changes can be made to it, but you will be allowed to annotate on it. This simply means that you will be able to use tools provided by the webtouch software to underline, write, draw, or use pointing devices. You are just sharing the file, and nothing else. So unlike sharing a desktop, if someone instant messages you, or you receive an email indicator with the subject line reading in bold "Happy Hour After Work...BE THERE", no one else will see it. Try and use file sharing whenever possible.

Application and Web Browser Sharing

Application sharing is similar to file sharing, but instead of loading in a file, you are actually allowing the attendees to view the application you are sharing. Application sharing is typically used when giving a demonstration of software, or changes to a file actually need to be made in your meeting. For example, when showing a piece of software you want your prospects to buy, you must show them all of the capabilities. It is also a best practice to hand over control to your prospect so they can get a hands-on experience. This is an extremely powerful way of engaging your prospect in the sale process and presentation.

Another example may be when sharing a contract with the signer and a few changes may need to be made. Are you starting to understand how powerful it can be to make the changes on the fly, with them as a part of the process? Gone are the days of emailing the contracts back and forth until everything is correct, and in are the days of doing this on-the-fly. Add the capability to transfer the final document to them via your webtouch selling tool and you have just significantly reduced your sales cycle. This, by the way, should become an integral part of your webtouch selling model. Maybe not presenting the contract at the same time of your initial presentation, but definitely using this tool for a contract review with your prospects.

Please note, your webtouch selling tools should also be smart enough to block, or at least mask incoming messages when sharing an application or web browser. If the tool is not equipped with this functionality, you may want to look elsewhere.

Desktop Sharing

Desktop sharing is the most self-explanatory of the sharing options your software will provide you. When you are sharing a desktop, you are sharing EVERYTHING on your desktop. This does include instant messages and email notifications that may popup. It is important to understand this when you do decide to share your desktop, and precautions may need to be made such as logging out of your messaging software, or turning off email notifications.

So if the file, application, and browser sharing seem to have all of the bases covered, then why would someone want to share a desktop? There are really only a couple of specific circumstances in which sharing your desktop may be used. For one, you may be hopping in and out of several applications in order to show someone how different things interact. For example, if the software you are giving a demonstration of integrates with some others, such as an email application, then desktop sharing may be the only way to effectively show this instead of sharing something, stopping the share, then choosing to share something else, etc. However, your webtouch tools provider may offer seamless bouncing between applications while actually in application share. You may want to verify this if needed.

Another example of when desktop sharing may be necessary is when performing "hands-on" support. Because passing control is usually a function available in desktop share, it is sometimes used to let someone grab control of a desktop for various reasons. However, the webtouch presentation tool is rarely used for this and we will focus on the support tool later in this book.

The Whiteboard

Sometimes in your online sales presentation it can make sense to use the whiteboard. When you share a whiteboard, a blank screen comes up in the viewing area of the presentation. The annotation tools, mentioned earlier, can then be used on your blank surface. Again, you should be allowed to type, freehand draw, use shapes, etc here all to help you make your point. Or, grant annotation controls to your prospect or customer to allow them to make theirs. This truly allows them to become involved in the meeting, and helps distinguish your sales pitch from someone else's! This helps put the "touch" in webtouch. Additionally, your software should allow you to save the whiteboard, usually as a .pdf file. Save it, file it in your prospect records, and/or send them a copy as part of follow-up. I'm telling you, this can really help you keep them in your sales process and bump someone else out!

File Transfer

File transfer functionality should be used whenever appropriate. If you are finished with your presentation, and your prospect needs some information in writing, be prepared to transfer it to them immediately in your online session. This will ensure that you both know they have it, and help reduce your sales cycle. Usually there is no cap on the size of the file, but make sure before you use so it is not an unsuccessful attempt in front of your prospect.

Using the File Menu to Transfer a File in Session

Choosing "Transfer" from the "File" menu will pull up a window allowing you to load content for participants to download.

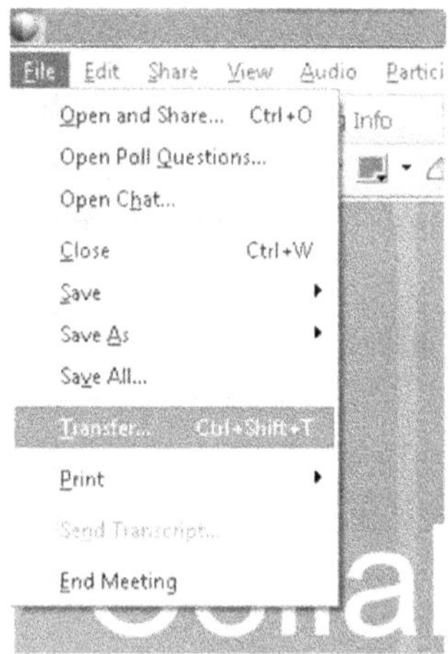

An In-session File Transfer Popup Window

This popup box will display all of the files you have loaded in for the participants to download. Indicators should let you know how many downloads are active, and once everyone is finished.

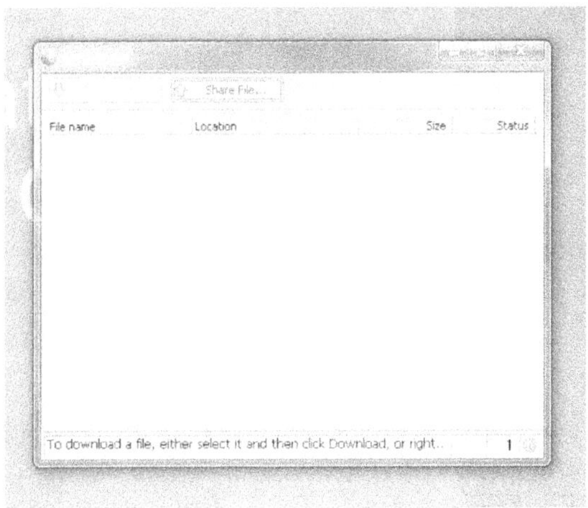

USING A WEBCAM

Video DOES make a difference! Even if you have a face made for radio, use your webcam to at least make introductions. If you don't, and your competing sales rep does, who do you think will make the lasting impression? It is not always the easiest thing to do, and practice makes perfect. There are quite a few sales reps I know that say the video helps them to ensure they are doing some of the little things that make a difference, such as smiling. And as we all know, body language can go a long way. So if your prospect asks a tough question, and you "show" them the confidence in your answer, they will feel better...guaranteed. Trust me, using your webcam will add integrity to you, your organization, and your presentation.

SHARING A PRE-RECORDED VIDEO

I write this next necessary section with a tad bit of caution. I say the section is necessary because organizations more and more want to show a pre-recorded video to their prospects. I write it with caution because this functionality is still in its infancy as the technology in general still has some catching up to do.

So what do I mean by a pre-recorded video? Sometimes just showing someone a slide depicting still images of something will not get your point across in the way in which you need. However, you feel the professionally done video you have stored on your computer will. This is evidenced in the growing use of websites such as YouTube for businesses to upload their videos in hopes their prospects will "find" them. A bit more powerful of an option however is to get your prospect in, and show it to them. So why would I not just share a web browser and take them to YouTube, or another hosting site? Their internal IT department may have those sites blocked (quite common), or the audio part of the video will not play on their end (also quite common).

The solution? Find webtouch selling software that will make this process a bit easier, and work effectively. If your software allows it, then it should be a separate option when clicking on "share" in your online meeting. For example, instead of choosing a slide deck or other file, choose your video from your computer. The idea is that your video will load into the viewing area, play effectively, and most importantly filter the audio portion through to your prospect as well. But again, this functionality seems to work best with certain file types and sizes. You may want or need to perform some backend work such as converting to certain file types to ensure video sharing is a success. If sharing videos is important, then you should definitely drill your webtouch tools provider and find out all you can about their capabilities. Additionally, some providers offer workarounds which can also be hit-or-miss. One thing is for certain...if you are planning on sharing pre-recorded videos in your presentation, then stick with the major providers of webtouch software.

Bringing your online presentation to a close

Closing down your webtouch presentation is technically very easy. You simply close the application as you would any other. But from a best-practice standpoint it is important to keep note of the fact that your presentation was probably quite different from your competitor's. So what can we do to make sure the final impression is a lasting one? There are several things.

A necessary best practice is to review what was discussed, and cover open "homework" for you, and hopefully them. Use the whiteboard here. This lets them know you truly listened to all of their concerns, and that you know what you need to do before following up. If you left something out here, they will tell you and you can then add it to the list. Also, list anything they said they would do before your next meeting. If they are finding out when their current contract expires with your competition, put it on the list. This lets them know you will hold them to it, and keeps them in your sales process even when not directly engaged...very powerful. Once your whiteboard is complete with tasks, save the file, and email it to them.

Another best practice is to ask them if they would like a recording of your meeting. Not only will this potentially let you know that they will be seriously reviewing some of the content of your meeting, but you can potentially monitor if and when they view it. Or, they may want to forward on the link to someone else who may be a key decision maker, but was unable to join your presentation. If they did not indicate this vital little piece of information early in your meeting, they may do it now. I would venture to say that this information is probably important to your sales pipeline and forecasting efforts.

Finally, I strongly encourage you to USE YOUR VIDEO again! Yes, flip it on once to say hi, and then flip it on again to say bye! The image of your smiling face waving goodbye via webcam will stick with your prospect...guaranteed! Look straight into the webcam, let them know you appreciate their time, and say goodbye!

Real World Example and Workflow - Software Sales Rep

Bruce is an Account Manager for ABC Solutions, a firm which sells medical records imaging software. While ABC is not the largest provider of imaging software, they are a key player in the market and one which their prospects should know by name.

The Challenge

Bruce has been losing more and more bids to a couple of his competitors. He has traditionally been very effective with his sales processes, and prides himself on his ability to speak effectively on the phone, and follow-up with information and meetings until his sales close. But recently he has figured out that his prospects are signing deals faster than usual, and with his competition. Bruce knows that their software is not necessarily any better than ABC's, and has a funny feeling they have a new sales tool...a tool which he has recently received his own login credentials for!

First Step

Bruce takes a look at a list of leads which has just been provided to him by his marketing team. While these are all good, quality leads generated from a recent webinar, Bruce decides to start at the top. His first call made reaches Shirley, the Office Manager at Wefix, Bones, and Associates (WBA). Shirley immediately explains that she is busy and does not have time for a sales pitch. Bruce lets her know he is simply trying to carve out a few minutes on the calendar in order to make an online presentation of their software. As Shirley still seems a bit weary, Bruce offers to overnight a gift card from a local coffee shop for an hour of her time on a Friday morning. Shirley now kindly accepts, and tells Bruce she will try and make sure she has Dr. Bones in the meeting as well, as he writes the checks. Bruce sets up the webtouch sales presentation through his email calendar, and emails Shirley the link to join Friday's meeting.

Friday Morning

Bruce has fired up his meeting a bit early, and pre-loads his presentation into the viewing area. His first slide not only shows his company's logo and information, but also WBA's. He feels this is a nice touch as organizations like to see their branding whenever and wherever they can. Bruce also pre-loads the whiteboard into the meeting, which shows up as a tab in the viewing area. This makes it easy for Bruce to jump from presentation to whiteboard and back if needed.

The meeting time rolls around, and Shirley joins on the hour. This is a great start as Bruce has been unable to have people stick to their telephone meetings recently. But things suddenly shift a bit when Shirley tells him that Dr. Bones called into the office this morning…something about an emergency golf outing. Instead of panicking, and feeling that his next hour could be a waste of breath, Bruce offers to record the meeting and provide Shirley a link which she can share with the Doc. Shirley is impressed, and said she will make sure he views it. Back on track.

Armed with a new webcam, Bruce clicks the "show video" button, and gives his introductions. Shirley is wowed by this, and says "well this is a nice change, being able to see who I am talking to!" Now that the mood is settled, Bruce flips off his camera, and shows the agenda slide he has created. Shirley mentions that she has a specific need, as well as a concern about some compliance issues…things not mentioned on his agenda slide. Bruce then jumps over to the whiteboard, and writes them in as important points to discuss.

We will assume now that the presentation went as planned, Bruce presenting his entire slide deck in the timeframe he mentioned, and covering all of Shirley's points. The presentation comes to an end with Bruce transferring Shirley a whitepaper on how ABC helps their customers meet their compliance requirements, and a copy of the whiteboard. Bruce also nails down a follow-up online meeting to review how WBA's internal discussions went, and cover any additional questions Dr. Bones may have. The other goal of the next online meeting will be to review the contract, and make any needed adjustments to pricing, terms, etc.

Flipping on the webcam again, Bruce thanks Shirley again for her time, and lets her know he is looking forward to the opportunity of working with HER (trying to gain her as a champion for his product). Yes, the online aspect, as well as live video truly makes this a more "intimate" working relationship...one that will separate ABC from their competition, and get them used to the webtouch selling process.

Chapter 7 The Online Training Tool – Keeping your Sales Teams Sharp and Knowledgeable

Now more than ever, it is important to get your teams the most up-to-date information in the fastest, most cost-effective ways possible. A well informed sales team, one in which everyone is on the same page, is a vital piece of your selling equation. If you are not sending a consistent message to your prospects and customers, someone else is.

So how do we ensure this speed of information delivery? We use the webtouch selling training application. Besides being an extremely inexpensive solution compared to potential travel costs, an effective online training application will deliver the information you need at the speed of the Internet. Again, all you need is a sales team with a computer, an Internet connection, a web browser, and a phone or VoIP setup.

Training your Team

We are going to make one main assumption in this section. We are assuming that you have multiple sales reps, and they are not centrally located. When we say centrally located, we mean in the same building, and usually on the same floor. In other words, if your sales team is easily brought into a single training room, then using an online training platform may just not make sense. If this is the case, then use that room to bring them in and train them on how to use the webtouch selling presentation tool!

Now that we have distinguished that your sales team does have multiple direct sales reps, and they are scattered around the city, state, country, and or globe, let's explore how the online training tool is used effectively.

Scheduling your Training

It is important to note that the interface for scheduling your training should be very similar to scheduling a webinar. You will probably access the scheduling interface the same way, and except for different options available to you, everything should basically look the same. However, since this section may be used as a reference for users of the training module only, we will be thorough and there may be some overlap.

First of all, let's login to the scheduling interface, and click on the "schedule a training" area. Here you will find all of the scheduling options which will "create" your online training session, and ultimately email all of the requested attendees a link for them to join. Let's start at the top, and review the typical options you will have for your session.

Session Information

In the session information area, you will usually just assign your training a title and password. The title will typically be the topic, and the password will be anything of your choosing. Typically there is not a need to get "crafty" with your password, as only the invited attendees will see it. Additionally, it is rare that outsiders will try and "hack" into your training session, and even if they did, you can always expel them once you see them in the participant's panel.

Other options in this area may include whether or not you want to list this training to the public, or make it private. As mentioned earlier, several of the webtouch selling software providers provide you a private URL for your services. In addition to being the administrative area, it is also the site in which attendees land in order to login to your training session. If the training is a private, internal training then perhaps you do not wish to list it publicly. However, if you are holding a larger training for your channel partners for example, then you would want to list it publicly.

Example: Let's say that you are offering several training sessions during a week span specifically for your channel partners. On your online training site you have listed 3 per day, for a 5 day period. In this situation you simply need to email the link to your training calendar to all of your partners, and let them browse times and dates, and register for the one which fits their availability.

Audio Options

This is the area in which you will decide how you want to handle the audio portion of your online training session.

Don't Forget!!

Remember, the audio piece of any webtouch selling solution is always the other part of the pricing equation.

There is usually a fixed price for the "license" or "host account", and then the audio is usually billed at a per-minute rate. The two main options you will have here are whether to use your existing audio conferencing provider, or use the audio provided by your webtouch software vendor.

If you have a vendor for your conferencing, such as AT&T, Verizon, Intercall, etc. then you should be able to input your conferencing bridge information into the settings of your training session. This information should then populate into the training invitation which your attendees will receive via email, making it very easy for them to join the web portion and audio portion.

However, you may have decided to use the audio conferencing services of your webtouch provider. This is actually very common when the training tool is being used because certain functionality is simply easier to use when the audio is already integrated together. Additionally, other features actually require that you use their audio in order to function correctly. These features can be things such as breakout sessions, attention indicators, active talker, and session recording. We will speak about all of these in the next few sections.

There may also be some other options listed for you to adjust in the audio area. Common things to look for here would be "muting" all participants upon entry into the meeting, displaying global call-in numbers, and requiring participants to have their name announced once they join. Remember, don't worry if you forget some of the audio details during your initial scheduling as you can usually change them in-session after it has been started.

VoIP as an Audio Option

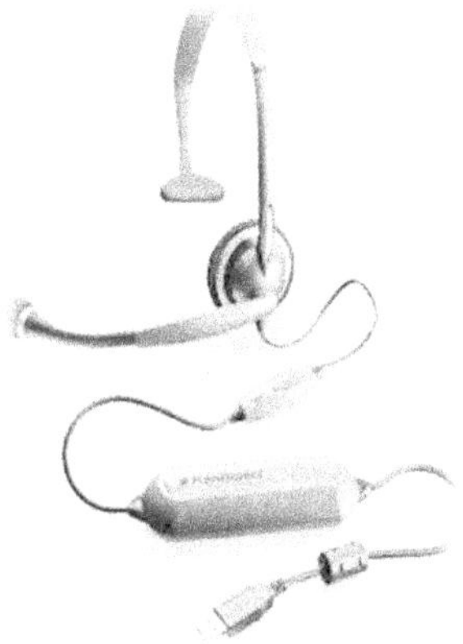

VoIP is an up and coming acceptable option for bridging the audio in online training sessions. For one, it is typically MUCH less expensive than using a traditional audio conferencing bridge. Second, more and more users are becoming comfortable with plugging in a headset to their computer. In order to use the VoIP functionality, users must have either a VoIP headset plugged in, or have speakers and a microphone. The headset option is the best way to go, as using just a microphone runs a risk of easily picking up background noise and interference.

The VoIP option should work just as any other audio option in the sense that all users can hear and speak. Additionally, most webtouch software providers offer this as a "hybrid" solution, simply meaning that some users call into the regular audio bridge, while others use VoIP, and everyone can communicate seamlessly. From the financial aspect of it, VoIP is sometimes included for free with the licensing package. If it is not included, it is usually less than a penny a minute. If your training sessions will continuously have the same people in them, then investing in a high quality VoIP headset for each user's computer will ultimately save you some serious money.

Training Date and Time

While the date and time of your training should be easy enough to figure out, we will cover a couple of options which can be used effectively. One option used often is the ability to allow attendees to join your training session before you actually start it. If you have never run late for anything in your life, and don't anticipate it ever happening, then don't worry about it. But for the rest of us, this is a very courteous gesture on your part! Allowing them to join the session before you start it not only allows you a bit of leeway if you are running late, but it also allows your participants time to make sure they don't run into any issues. These issues are not necessarily related to your session itself, but could be on the user's end if they are joining an online event for the first time.

This section might also allow you to setup the training as recurring (as in the one week example listed previously), or as a multiple-session course in which participants may be required to attend several. Take a look around here in your evaluation of the training software, and make sure these options fit into your training initiatives.

Participant Registration

The main option you can choose in the registration area is whether or not to require your participants to register for the training session. If you choose to not require registration, then participants will be able to join by submitting the most basic of information, such as their name and email address. For online training sessions this is not very common as the information you want to gather from them is almost as important as the information you will be presenting. However, if you don't need it, then don't include it.

More often than not however you will want to require your participants to register for your training. Besides this function enabling you to know beforehand who will be joining, it also allows you to access registration reports both before and after your training session. When you do require registration, you should have the ability in your software to customize the registration form. So in addition to gathering their name and email address, you may want to know their employee ID, what their exact job title is, who their manager is, or even what company they are from if you are training your channels. Be creative here as all of these fields should populate to the registration reports you will eventually access for your records.

An additional option typically found in the registration area is the ability to automatically approve all registrants. This is a handy feature which prevents you from having to manually approve, or deny registrants as they submit their registration information. Once approved, they should receive their unique registration ID in their confirmation email, which will be required for them to join.

However, you may want to play gatekeeper on your training sessions. By not automatically approving registrations, you will receive an email each and every time someone registers which should include all of the information you required them to put in. You can then approve them, deny them, or even let them know their registration is pending. This can be an important feature to use if your training session is one in a series of other training sessions. You may require that they have completed one, or even several other classes before they have the right to join another one.

Example: You have setup a weeklong series of online training classes for your sales team which will cover a variety of new enhancements to your software. As a firm understanding of the new interface is needed before they learn about other new features and functionality, it is important for them to have completed the interface training before moving on. While you may not necessarily deny them from joining the latter trainings, it is important for you to know that they did not complete the first one. Or, when you receive Mike's registration request for the 3rd session, only to see he has not completed the first two, perhaps you require him to at least view the recordings of the first two sessions before approving him for the third.

There are many, many examples in which the registration approval functionality can be of benefit to you. Focus a little bit here on what is important for your training initiatives, and make certain your software offers this feature, if needed.

ATTENDEES

This section of the scheduling is where you will input your participants email addresses in order to have the software send out the invites. Usually you will be able to simply type in their email addresses, separated by commas or semicolons, or even upload a file of email addresses for larger training sessions.

PRESENTERS

Your webtouch selling software will usually distinguish between attendees (participants) and Presenters. The difference here is that your presenters will typically show up in a separate panel in the training session, and have different privileges than the participants. For example, you can assign a certain Presenter the right to field the Question & Answer panel in the meeting, or allow participants to send private chat or questions specifically to that Presenter. Additionally, if it is a guest speaker, it is important to have them distinguished from the crowd.

Breakout Sessions

Breakout sessions are THE answer to preventing "death-by-PowerPoint", and help ensure retention of your information. In short, a breakout session gives you the ability to "break out" participants into smaller groups. So just as if we were in an in-person training session, and our trainer were to break us into small groups to collaborate, the breakout feature in your online training software "virtually" does the same thing.

"Death-by-PowerPoint" is a term used to describe what happens to your group when you simply present information to them and "ask" them to retain it. You will keep their attention for the first few slides, then lose it for the majority of your presentation, and then (if they are not asleep) hopefully gain it again at the end. This is not an effective way of training, and the participant's retention of your information greatly suffers.

The breakout session functionality in your webtouch software will allow you to break up the monotony of your presentation by sending your participants out into smaller sessions. Typically, a Host will automatically be chosen for their breakout sessions, meaning they have control of that smaller session and can share documents, applications, the whiteboard, etc. The Host role can be changed once in the session if needed. The main Host, as well as other presenters and/or panelists, of the larger training session should have the ability to drop into each of the smaller meetings and ask questions, provide feedback, offer guidance, and whatever else they deem fit. After the allotted time of the breakout session, with a click of the mouse the main Host can then bring everyone back into the meeting, and the large training session is back in motion.

In addition to breaking up the monotony of the meeting, the breakout sessions will lead to a higher retention of the information you are delivering. If a participant is part of a large training without breakout sessions, they may wander off and surf the web, check email, or make phone calls. The risk is low here as they do not assume they will be called on for anything. However, if they know they will be broken out into a smaller group with their peers, they are more apt to pay attention so they do not embarrass themselves in the small group.

Remember, it is easier to hide in a larger group than a smaller one!

Please note that usually breakout sessions can be created before your training sessions, or even on the fly once the training session has begun.

Breakout Session Setup Screenshot

Breakout sessions can be created during the scheduling process, or on-the-fly. Below is an example of the window that will appear when scheduling a breakout session once the meeting has started.

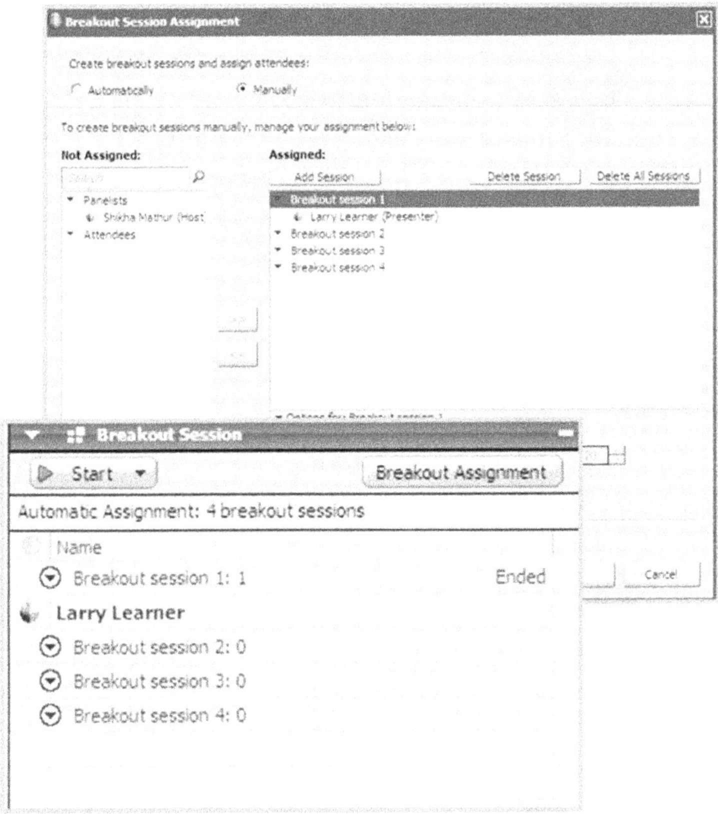

ATTENTION INDICATORS (THE BIG BROTHER FEATURE!)

This is a newer feature in some online training software, but an important one. The attention indicator can be seen usually by the Host and/or Presenters only, and appears as a mark next to a participant's name when they are viewing something on their computer other than your presentation. So if Johnny has a red exclamation mark next to his name, you know he may not be paying attention. Or, if the mark is appearing next to multiple participants' names, you may be losing the group as a whole and it is time for a break, or a breakout session! You may also find that your webtouch provider indicates this information in the reporting functionality, meaning that after your session you can run a report which will indicate the exact percentage of time the training presentation was in the forefront of their computer!

Tip: Is one of your sales representatives struggling and telling you it is due to lack of training? Show them that they in fact do not pay attention to the training you provide! If needed, file this report away in their employee file.

Attention Indicators Screenshot

In this screenshot, the attention indicators are the exclamation points. They show that Heather and Liz are doing something other than paying attention to the session.

Other Session Options

This section will allow you to choose which other options you want to include, or not include in your training sessions. These options are usually the panels which will show up to the right of the presentation area. Popular options here include:

- Polling – the ability to pose a question to the group, along with multiple choice answers. These polling results can then be broadcast to the group. Polling can come in handy when you want to "engage" your audience, or even just to gather the retention of your latest information. Use this feature to also determine if you should move on to the next topic, or spend a little more time hammering home the message.
- Video – If offered by your provider, the video option will allow you to use a webcam to broadcast your video. If your software offers a multi-point video option, then your participants will be able to broadcast their video as well. We will look a bit more about how the video can be used in the real-world example at the end of this chapter.
- Chat – This panel is just as it sounds...a chat area inside your meeting. Privileges can be assigned to participants allowing them to chat with everyone, or with just Presenters. Keep in mind that participants can usually chat privately amongst themselves as well. Enable the chat functionality in your training sessions wisely, and instead look to use the Q & A functionality.

Session Question and Answer (Q & A)

This feature is perhaps the most commonly used panel in an online training session. While it is very similar to the chat panel, it is different in a major way. If you have an online training session going with let's say 50 people, the chances are high that multiple chats will come in at the same time. This is a nightmare for anyone trying to answer the chats, and almost impossible to manage. Your Q & A panel should offer "threading". Threading simply means that the Presenter who is managing the Q & A only needs to click on the question, and then type in the answer. The answer will show up in the Q & A panel directly beneath the question it pertains to. You should also be able to go to the File menu, and save the Q & A as a text file. This gives you a file of all of the questions and answers from your training session which you can email out to all participants, or even post on your website.

Course Material

You may find it important to provide certain materials to your training class before the actual live session. This can be accomplished by dropping files into the course material area, which can then be downloaded once the registrant either registers, or receives their login credentials.

Testing

What is a good training session without a test at the end? You may have a large sales team and need to figure out which members will be getting the best leads for your new software offering. After providing a week's worth of training, a test can quickly establish which sales reps are most worthy of the golden leads. The testing engine allows you to attach a test to the end of the live session. If you choose to create only multiple choice and true/false questions, then the testing engine should actually grade the test automatically, and forward you the results. Of course you can also add essay, short answer, and other types of questions, but you will be responsible for grading those manually.

Testing Screenshots

Explore some of the options below in one provider's included testing engine.

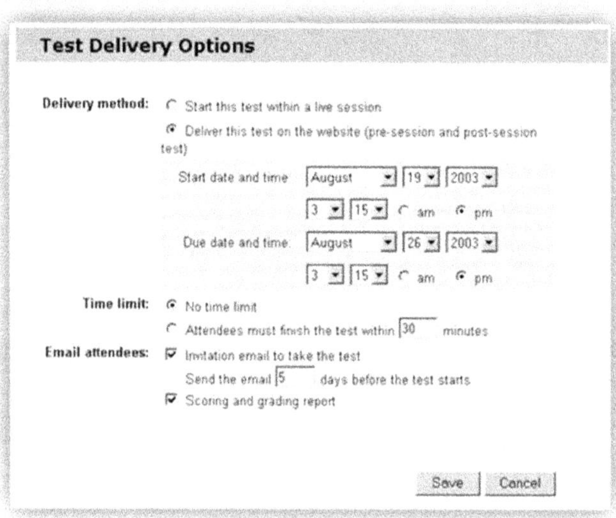

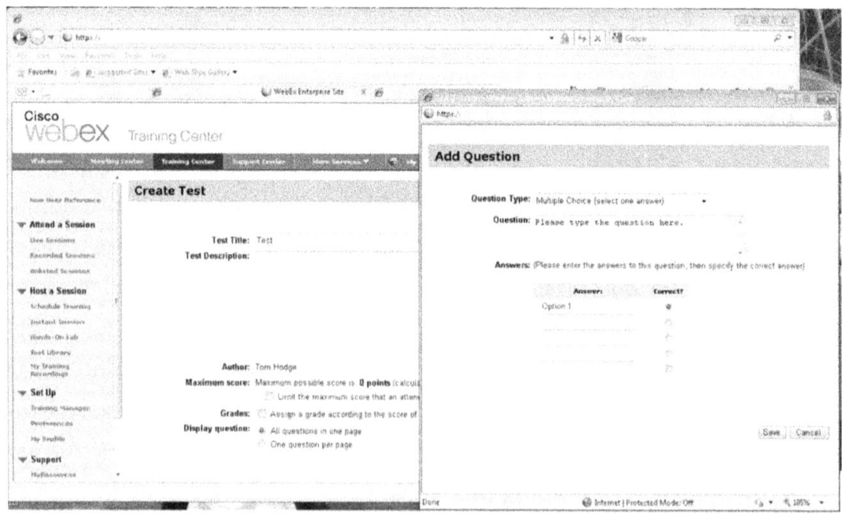

Real World Example and Workflow

The Challenge

Your software company, NoBugs, Inc., is about to release its newest version to the market. In addition to a brand new interface, there are many other enhancements and functionality for the end user, as well as technical specifications which close up several security holes. As your sales team is responsible not only for sales, but also for providing demos and talking through the new fixes, it is important to get everyone up to speed. Time is of the essence here, as your main competitor ZeroBugs, Llc. is slowly encroaching into your market and taking away some of your customers. Additionally, they seem to be staffed with some additional engineers who can speak more technically, and your budget does not include the ability to add this higher level of subject matter expert. So what do you do?

You have created your training curriculum and decided that you need about 15 hours to effectively present everything to your sales team. So to begin, you schedule a week-long training program using your newly acquired webtouch training tool, and block off 3 hours a day for the sessions. All of your in-session options are set and you send out the invitations to the sales team. Luckily enough, you have been able to also invite your head software engineer and add her as a Presenter so that she will be able to field Q & A.

You will be using several new terms throughout your training, and instead of spending time in-session trying to go over them, you provide a glossary-of-new-terms in the course material section. This will allow everyone to download the content beforehand and help ensure no one gets lost at the outset.

Additionally, because you will be using breakout sessions, you choose to use your webtouch provider's audio for ease of use, and tight integration. You also do not want anyone chatting privately amongst themselves, so you set the chat privileges to allow participants to only chat with the Host or Presenters.

Because your sales team is only 30 people strong, you feel that you can easily handle the registration requests coming in, so you choose not to have it done automatically. While you have no intention of preventing anyone from registering for any of the sessions, you do wish to know if they have missed any of them. You have also chosen to record each of your sessions so in case someone does need to miss one, they can catch up to the group by viewing the recording when their time permits. These recordings will also help with any new hires which need to be brought up to speed!

The first day of training is focusing on the new user interface. After spending about 30 minutes doing your own pointing and clicking around, you start to see the attention indicators popping up, and decide it is a perfect time for a breakout session. You announce to the group that you will be breaking them into six groups of five, and they need to elect a group spokesperson.

The goal of the breakout session is for the group leader (breakout Host) to share the software, and pass control around to the group. There are 5 main functions in which each team member needs to perform with the software, and provide feedback. The group leader will use the whiteboard to list their top 5 thoughts or questions on the new interface. After 20 minutes, you will bring everyone back into the training session, and the group leader will click on the "raise hand" icon indicator.

Now that everyone is back in the main training room, you will call on each of the group leaders to share the results. You begin by asking them to flip on their webcam so everyone can see them, and then pass them presenter privileges so they can write on the group whiteboard. After all group leaders have presented, you open it up for discussion by unmutung anyone who clicks on the raise hand icon. You are now an hour or so into your training, and your team is starting to "get" it. They should also now understand how important it is for them to pay attention!

The above shows a session flow which can be duplicated over and over again, and will therefore suffice for the remaining of this week. So let's jump to the end of the training session, and create a test so we can assess our training initiatives.

You have already decided that your time is better spent NOT grading tests, so you opt to keep it as simple as possible, while still getting you the results you need. Thoughts are that 20 multiple choice and true/false questions will be adequate, and so you use the included testing engine to create it. At the end of the last live training session, you inform the group that once you shut down the training, a test will automatically appear on their screen. They will have one hour to complete it, and if they are successful then they can immediately begin calling on current customers and look for upsell opportunities. You now simply need to sit back, and view their test results which get emailed to you!

Chapter 8 The Support Tool – Elevating your Customer's Support Experience

Transactional revenue is of course a wonderful thing, but so are upsells, repeat sales, and recurring revenue. High customer satisfaction, loyalty, and retention are crucial ingredients to long-term growth. And it goes without saying that any organization's absolute best prospects are the ones which have already purchased from them.

There are a lot of challenges presented to organizations when it comes to supporting its customers. Many include the following:

- Customer satisfaction and retention
- Regulation and compliance relating to interactions with customers
- Skyrocketing customer service expenses
- Recognizing possible upsell opportunities

Having the tools in place to assist with these challenges is easy by implementing this tool in the webtouch selling suite.

Customer Satisfaction and Retention

The webtouch support application is used to deliver high-touch online support to your most valuable customers. The tool will be used by the members of the sales team who are dedicated to the support related issues. While the tool immediately shows itself to be invaluable to any technical support environment, its contents under the hood can greatly empower any customer service team which fields requests via phone and/or web. The abilities for a support group to take a website request and elevate it to an online chat, then to a direct phone call, then to a full-blown sharing session, are enhancing company's support initiatives almost overnight. Although usually considered the "tail-end" application in a webtouch selling model, it can also be considered the "glue" that keeps your customers in tune with your webtouch selling model, and comfortable with your webtouch model!

Solving Regulation and Compliance Issues

Most organizations realize the importance of adhering to their customer's needs in a timely and effective manner. Some organizations are bound by industry regulation, while others are bound by their own internal Service Level Agreements and Statements of Support. In addition to being an effective way of providing immediate support, the webtouch support tool allows the organization to "comply" through its ability to record and document the interactions. A Support Representative simply needs to record the meeting, add some notes, and file the recording away in the customer file. This simple, yet powerful process can save an organization significant amounts of time and money associated with handling customer complaints and/or industry audits.

Keeping Support Related Expenses low and measurable

The costs involved with acquiring the webtouch support software and training the reps are minimal. Costs involved with NOT implementing this piece of the webtouch selling process can be maximal. Direct, cost related benefits include:

- Reduced average hold time
- Shortened average request handling time
- Increases speed to resolution
- Solidifies retention, and re-ordering

Used effectively, this tool will fine-tune your support initiatives, help keep support related expenses at a minimum, and allow the support reps to focus on opportunities for upsells.

Recognizing Upsell Opportunities

The best customer is a happy customer. By providing a level of support which is higher than your competition, you can ensure that your customers stay put, and keep buying. Customer Support representatives can be trained on the basics of what to look for when it comes to selling your customers some additional services, and easily make a transition to your webtouch sales rep for the presentation. If your customer is used to the webtouch level of support, they are extremely likely to agree to a follow-up web presentation from your sales team.

How Does the Tool Work?

Of all the webtouch selling tools, this is the one which typically has a slightly different interface, and doesn't usually allow you to pre-schedule meetings. After all, the support tool is usually used to handle support requests on-the-fly, as no one really knows that they will need help in the future! In order to illustrate how this software can help your webtouch selling model, we will dig right into a couple of real world examples and workflows.

Example 1 – A Software Company

You have effectively been selling your new and improved software to customers, but now are starting to field calls with support related questions. Traditionally, your support reps have fielded the calls out of a queue, and then attempted to answer questions and provide help without the ability to see what the customer is seeing. This has led to inaccurate support, elevated complaints, increases in support response times, and overall decreasing customer satisfaction levels. Emergency meetings have been called to let everyone know that while revenues have been increasing, retention is dropping. The net effect is bad for business continuation.

What can be Done?

As the head of your customer support team, you decide to revamp the support area of your website. Instead of the first option of support being the telephone number for customers to call, you decide to add a WebACD icon. WebACD stands for Web Automated Call Distribution. When clicked by someone looking for support, a box pops up on their screen asking them to choose one of several potential problems they may be having. Once they submit their issue, the request is immediately routed to one of the five support folks on your team letting them know that someone needs help associated with their expertise. If that person is busy, the customer can be notified of the approximate wait time, and go into a holding queue.

WebACD

Below is an icon which can be added to the help area of your website. Clicking on it will typically pull up an option box for the customer to choose the type of help they need, and then immediately connect them with a support rep for a chat session.

The below screenshot shows an example workflow of a customer clicking for help, moving into a queue, and then being connected with the appropriate support representative.

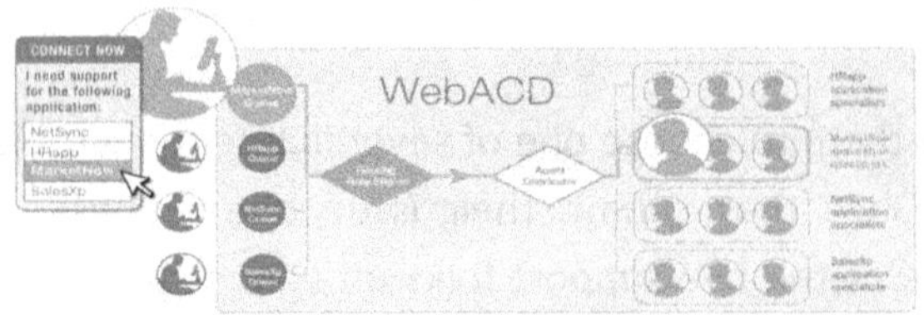

Once the customer's time has come, your support rep can immediately engage in an online chat session and attempt to answer the questions. A click-to-call function also allows the support rep to talk to the customer on the phone, while not requiring the customer to listen to your horrible hold music. Additionally, some of the webtouch software providers will even allow your support rep to send a video stream via their webcam. Believe it or not, this has proven to calm the customer down a bit as the support session now has a more personal feel to it.

Sometimes this chat session and phone call will do the trick, and everyone is happy. But other times, there may need to be some escalation. Your webtouch support tool should allow you to immediately elevate the chat session into a full-blown desktop share so that your support rep can see your customer's computer screen, and everything they are doing. To add, your support rep should also be able to take control of your customer's computer if necessary.

What you should be left with is a customer that is happy that they received such a high level of support in such a timely manner. People don't always like to have to pick up the phone, and they definitely do not like to listen to hold music. This webtouch support is a much more personal, and efficient way of handling your customers, and should help you keep them around.

Example 2 - A Financial Services Firm

A bank has recently updated their website to reflect a portfolio of newly offered CD's. In order to try and capture interested customers and prospects more effectively, they have included a "click-to-chat" icon on the website. This click-to-chat icon is an out-of-the box feature found with some of the webtouch selling support application.

Customer A is now on the website, and has some questions about the different rates and terms available. They click on the chat icon, and are immediately connected with a Financial Specialist from the bank. The chat is going well, but in order to add some personalization to the session, the FS elevates the session to a phone call as well. Impressed with this level of support and attentiveness, the prospect begins to ask questions related to paperwork required for making a deposit. Instead of the traditional method of sending out information, the FS decides to engage in a full-blown web meeting and share out their desktop.

Now that the session is fully interactive, and a true webtouch experience for the prospect, the FS has greater control of the outcome of the call. Feeling that this is a good time to move forward, the FS shares a deposit form on their screen, and fills it out with the prospect. Now that all of the paperwork is completed, the prospect simply needs to come into the bank and sign on the dotted line. This entire experience may have taken only a few minutes, and may have gained the bank significant deposits.

Summary

The examples laid out here show not only how the webtouch selling support tool will add high levels of support to your organization's efforts, but also how it can be used to directly lead to sales. The next time these customers have a need for services, they are highly more likely to return to the same source than through a competitor!

Chapter 9 The Enterprise Instant Messaging Tool – Keeping your Support Team and Subject Matter Experts only a Click Away

GONE are the days of "Let me find that answer and get back to you"!

What is an Enterprise Instant Messaging tool?

Instant Messaging tools have been around since America Online became a household name and people began using the World Wide Web. The only thing we really mean by adding the term "Enterprise" is that these tools have come a long way, and are now being offered with features that businesses are looking for.

Because there are a lot of instant messaging tools out there, and because they are usually free and very easy to use, employees have started to download and use their own preferred versions. In an attempt to calm the nerves of IT staffs, and get all employees on the same platform, the providers of webtouch selling software have added an Instant Messaging tool to the mix. This gives the employees what they need to communicate, and also allows the IT department to maintain control of their environments. But beyond the IT benefits of a single EIM tool, it is PRICELESS in its usefulness to a sales team.

An Instant Messaging Interface

In this example, all contacts are listed in a single group, and only a click away. Most EIM tools will offer similar functionality, and are vital to maintaining a high level of availability for the sales team and support folks.

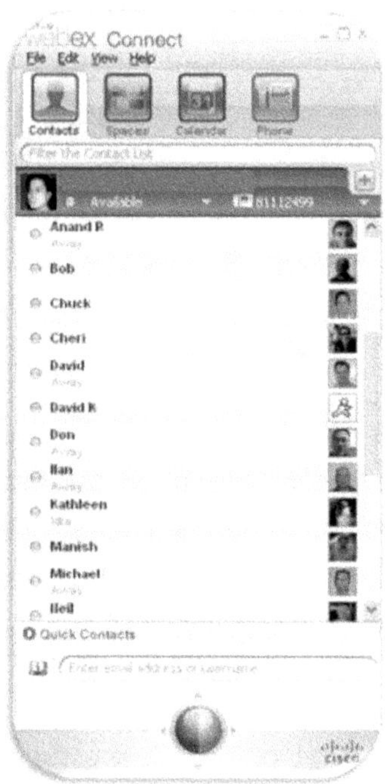

ANSWERS ARE ONLY A CLICK AWAY!

Before the days of being equipped with the EIM tool, sales reps would prolong a sales cycle when trying to track down answers to questions posed by prospects and customers. Depending on the response time internally by a subject matter expert, potential sales could literally dissolve if the competition got the answers before you. But now answers to those questions can be instantaneous.

When I get in the office every morning, I fire up my EIM tool before email. The order doesn't really matter, but the point of its importance needs to be noted. It has become an extremely rare occurrence that I would need to let my prospect off the hook while I track down additional information. Just as you may be used to separating your "buddy list" into friends, family, etc., your EIM tool will allow you to do the same. Except in our world they are separated by product, service, or any other internal role the contacts play. For example...when a customer asks me the exact bandwidth used when someone is broadcasting video over a shaped T1, I am clueless. But Joe Engineer, who is 3,000 miles away from me, can answer my question immediately! This helps my credibility, puts my prospect at ease, and keeps my sales cycle as short as possible.

Keeping your channel reps just as close

Not only will the EIM tool be used to keep everyone close internally, but it will also be used to better communicate with your channel partners. Most of the EIM tools are built on a technology called XMPP. This simply means that they are built with an underlying technology which allows different tools from different vendors to effectively communicate with each other. So even though I am using my company's webtouch selling software, I can add a partner to my contact list as long as their EIM tool is built on the XMPP platform

In addition to having different internal contacts grouped accordingly, I also have my channel partners grouped in my EIM list. This is a great way for me to maintain that webtouch model with the other people selling my products. If we are working on a deal together, and they need my assistance to help them close a deal, I am only a click away. Not only that, all of my resources are only a click away as well. If one of my partners is engaged in an opportunity and needs immediate help, they can get it quickly. And guess who's products that partner is more likely to sell knowing that they have this level of support and availability to resources???

KEEP YOUR CUSTOMERS EVEN CLOSER!

Hopefully you have now begun to see how an EIM tool can help you easily get questions answered, keep your sales cycle short, and stay in front of others selling your products. But what about your customers? Now you may want to tread a little lightly here as having your customers be able to ping (a term used for instant messaging someone) you at will may not be the best idea. But depending on who the customer is, this may prove to be the best idea in the world.

A typical rule of thumb may be to only establish these direct connections with your best customers. It s certainly a level of support your competitor is probably NOT offering. And if it turns out that they are taking advantage of the access you have given them, and bombard you with unnecessary questions, then maybe they aren't your best customer! But I can tell you from experience that the few of my largest customers I do have IM connections with sincerely appreciate it, only ping me when necessary, and a lot of times it is to discuss more of our offerings!

Again...the Enterprise Instant Messaging piece of the webtouch selling suite is becoming one of the most important. If your organization can step away from the stigma of an instant messaging tool being for fun and games, and instead see the value it can bring to your sales efforts, then it will see immediate benefits of implementing it. Not all webtouch selling software providers offer this type of tool. If they do, chances are high that it integrates with their entire suite of webtouch selling software. Benefits of this include:

- the ability to elevate from a messaging session to a full-blown web meeting

- the capability to invite others into a currently funning session directly from the chat interface, and
- see the availability of others through presence indicators (the EIM tool usually syncs with the employee's calendar, phone, or both)

So even though you may choose a webtouch software provider that does not provide this tool, you may want to implement this tool separately through another vendor.

Part IV – An Insider's Guide to Understanding the Vendor Environment, Available Pricing Models, and Getting the most for your Money

Chapter 10 Understanding the Vendor Environment

You MUST understand the rules of the game before you can play to win!

WHO SHOULD I BE TALKING WITH TO ACQUIRE WEBTOUCH SELLING SOFTWARE?

The big names should already be evident. Based only on market share as given by Synergy research, here is a list of the main companies you would want to consider:

- CISCO WebEx
- CITRIX GoTo
- Microsoft

While the above are the big gorillas in the room, the following companies should also be noted as providing webtouch selling solutions:

- Adobe
- IBM
- iLinc
- Saba

All of the companies listed above are the actual companies who provide their own branded solutions. But webtouch selling software can also be purchased from Service Providers. We are about to dig much deeper so that you will fully understand how this all works, but note these key Service Providers before we move forward:

- Intercall
- AT&T
- Verizon
- Global Crossing
- Premiere Global
- Arkadin

Let's further add some confusion to the mix by letting you know you can also purchase from channel partners (resellers) of the Direct Providers. These channel partners are typically located in the same geographic region as your company headquarters, and probably help supply your company with other technology products and/or services. The chances are very high that your company already has a relationship with a local IT services firm so understanding how they fit into the mix is also very important. Some of the following companies are names to look for (there is no way we can cover all of them as there are literally THOUSANDS of them):

- CDW
- Presidio
- INX
- Coleman Technologies

The Gartner Magic Quadrant for Web Conferencing (Gartner, 2010)

Gartner is a 3rd party organization offering objective insight into over 1,071 topics across the IT landscape. Below is their report on the web conferencing providers.

Source: Gartner (November 2010)

WOW, THAT WAS A LOT OF INFORMATION…PLEASE GUIDE ME

At first glance, the above information can seem a bit confusing. Especially if you have just Googled "web conferencing providers"! You have probably seen many different results returned, including companies not even listed above. This is because there are literally HUNDREDS of smaller companies out there vying for a piece of the enormous pie that is web conferencing. That is what makes this chapter SO important to read and understand before taking the plunge.

Direct Providers

First let us define a Direct Provider (DP) as the company that you can purchase services directly from. For example, you can call CISCO, CITRIX, or Microsoft and be connected with the area Account Manager who is in charge of selling their webtouch selling software in the geographical region in which your company is headquartered. You are buying directly from them, and therefore they are the DP.

Going straight to the DP is by far the most common way of acquiring your webtouch selling tools. Not only are you cutting out any "middlemen", but you have direct access to these large company's resources. Additionally, the timeframe for actually getting your service activated and setup can be drastically reduced as the Account Manager usually has direct access to their internal resources. But other situations may dictate that your organization acquires webtouch selling software from other means...let's take a look.

DP's Channel Partners (Resellers)

At the time of this writing, acquiring webtouch selling software through a reseller is becoming a very popular way of purchasing. Partners can purchase the software on your behalf, mark it up a bit, and resell it to you. If your organization has more than around 100 employees, then the chances are pretty high that it has a relationship with a local, regional, or national reseller of the major IT companies. The main reason for this is that the major IT companies prefer to maintain a model in which their core products are sold through these channels, rather than direct. For example, CISCO Systems probably sells 98% of their products through channels. Trying to purchase something directly from CISCO (other than webtouch selling software) is darn near impossible. To compare, imagine calling SONY directly to purchase a TV...not gonna happen!

Because these large companies prefer to distribute products and services through their channels, they typically offer incentives. These incentives are in the form of a lower price to your organization's partner...consider it wholesale. So if your organization has a good relationship with a partner, then you can probably trust that they will not mark up the webtouch selling software beyond what is reasonable. Additionally, they may even be able to offer you a pricing package which is not even available by going directly to the source. We will look a bit more at this when it comes to pricing and negotiating your services.

Another advantage in purchasing your tools through a partner is that the partner is usually located close to your organization. Check with your IT department to verify this, and get their input. If your partner is located locally, they can usually offer an added level of support. I think it is important to note however that in my experiences they usually don't add a lot of value when it comes to setting up or using the webtouch selling tools. The main value they can bring to the table is help with integrating other communications equipment you may have in your organization. For example, your company may have an internal communications or audio conferencing infrastructure which you want to use on top of your web conferencing. This would be an alternative to paying for audio by the minute. Instead, your company has invested in its own equipment to handle the audio portion of your conferencing. Integrating that equipment with your webtouch selling software can, and usually should be handled by these partners.

Service Providers

The third way to acquire webtouch selling software is through a Service Provider. As mentioned earlier, these companies include the likes of AT&T, Verizon, Intercall, and Premiere Global. Service Providers are usually partnered with your organization already and supply it with other communications services. These services mainly include the backbones which allow you to use your telephones and connect your company to the Internet. These companies also offer audio conferencing, as well as web conferencing. Kind of like a partner, they acquire the software directly from the software providers, mark it up, and resell it to you. You can usually negotiate rates with them for all of your conferencing needs, including the webtouch selling software.

Using your Service Provider definitely has its advantages, as well as its disadvantages. Key advantages can include the ability to leverage your existing relationship to negotiate pricing and terms (we will dig much deeper into this shortly). But disadvantages can include the simple fact that they need to mark up the services in order to make their profit, and from a technology standpoint some of them simply "piggyback" you onto their system. Depending on the SP, they may be on a system which is not the most up-to-date and therefore have you on software which is not providing the latest features which you may need. It is also important to note that certain features and functionality may not work as easily as they would if you go directly to the source. Things like recording, muting and unmutung of attendees, breakout sessions, and active talker may not work correctly. Make sure you cover all of your bases.

Summary

As you have read, there are numerous ways to purchase your webtouch selling software. And as your IT department will probably be involved at some point in the acquisition process, they may be able to help guide you towards the best source. Purchasing directly is substantially more popular of a choice for organizations which have less than 250 employees. If your organization has more than 250, while purchasing directly is still by far the more popular way, you may find that utilizing other sources may be more beneficial or even mandated internally. The next chapters on pricing structures and terms may ultimately be the best way for you to determine which way to go.

Chapter 11 Understanding the different pricing models, and contract terms available

The main point to remember while reading the next sections is that there are really only 3 main pricing models from all of the providers...licenses, minutes, and ports.

In this chapter, we will help transform the extremely complex into something very simple. Pricing of webtouch selling software and services can be very tricky. In fact, it is typically the last piece of training the Account Managers receive and usually takes several months for them to get a firm grasp on it (trust me on this one...we all still help each other and we have been doing this for a long time). Being armed with prior knowledge of what you are up against is key. In this chapter we will break it all down, and provide you with some of the absolute best information from an insider's prospective. If read and understood, this chapter can save you bukoo bucks!

Individual Licenses, Named Hosts, User Accounts, etc.

By far the most popular way to price webtouch selling software is by individual license. These can also be termed Named Hosts, User Accounts, User Licenses, etc. The idea is that if an employee needs the ability to schedule and run an online session, they need a license. What makes this so popular is that it is easy to understand, and is a fixed cost.

Pricing for licenses is usually straightforward enough. There is a flat fee per license which allows that user to run as many meetings as they want. The meter is not running with this pricing model, which makes it easy for budgeting and forecasting purposes. Additionally, the vendor should offer discounts based on the number of licenses you purchase. These breakpoints will be different depending on company, so make sure you at least ask. We will cover best practices for these negotiations shortly.

The "Minutes" Model

The "minutes" model is the second most popular pricing model. What really makes it popular is the flexibility. What makes it unpopular is that the meter is running when someone is hosting a meeting.

When you decide to go with a minutes model, you are purchasing a bucket of data minutes for all of your users to use. This allows you to login to the administrator area, and create user accounts for any number of employees...there is no limit. This can be a good model for you if you want to give access to many different users, but you are unsure of just how much they will use it. For example, you may have some employees who only need to run a meeting, training, or webinar once every couple or few months. Purchasing them an individual license may seem unnecessary, and prove to be more expensive than just letting them dip into the bucket of minutes.

But this model can also become VERY expensive. If you have some users doing a lot of online presentations, then they are using a lot of minutes. Additionally, the minutes model would be a TERRIBLE idea for large webinars or trainings...can you imagine? We have done the math for you, and come up with the following rule of thumb:

- If you have a user doing at least one online presentation per month, GET THEM A LICENSE!

Now, of course you may be in a situation where you are just beginning to implement your webtouch selling model, and are not yet sure who the main users will be. You are also not sure just how much it will be used. Your anticipations are high, but you're not certain yet. This is where you can explore a "hybrid" model.

THE "HYBRID" MODEL

We mentioned that there are really three main pricing models...this is not one of them. For simplicity sake we will just let you know that this is a blend of the two most popular. Here is the situation, and how it can work:

Let's say you have a team of 15 sales reps and you want to transition them over to a webtouch selling model. Your marketing, training, and/or support folks already have individual licenses because that is what makes sense. But you feel moving all 15 sales folks over will take a bit of time, and your budget is tight. You know for a fact the 5 of them will adopt immediately, as they have used the tool before at other jobs. But what about the other 10?

Start by purchasing individual licenses for the 5 reps who you know will use it. Add a bucket of minutes so that the other 10 will have access, but you won't be overpaying if they are not using them. What will happen is that your "power users" will begin to emerge. Once you see a rep using the tool effectively, purchase them a license. Ultimately you will have everyone moved over to licenses, and you can cancel the minutes. Keep this strategy in mind when you are negotiating terms for the minutes portion of your contract. And yes...different services on the same account CAN have different terms. We will cover more in depth later.

Ports Model

This is a slightly antiquated pricing structure and rarely found, or even offered anymore. This was the original way that the webtouch selling software providers offered their services, and it used to make a bit more sense. But as the popularity of webtouch selling has drastically increased, so have the pricing options.

Another term for ports is "seats", or "connections". For example, if you purchase 10 ports, then you can have a total of 10 connections at any given time...and no more. So if you have one person running a presentation with 9 attendees, no one else can run a meeting or presentation while this one is running. Or if you have 2 people with 4 attendees each, then the same thing applies. You are always limited to the number of ports you have...no flexibility.

Is there any situation in which you should consider ports? The answer is yes. Nowadays an individual license will typically allow up to 25 total attendees. And this is where they start. Ports are expensive, and to buy 25 of them would cost you about 50 times as much as the individual license. However, you must remember that the license is assigned to one individual user. The software companies do not want these licenses shared, and will play hardball with you if they suspect it is happening. This is where ports can actually be of benefit. Let's take a look at the following example:

You have a conference room which you have dedicated to use for web presentations to your best prospects and customers. You have equipped this "selling room" with a high quality webcam, phone system, and background scenery. The idea is that you need to be able to give many different people access to this room, but only when needed. The meetings or presentations will be very small, and very intimate. In order to keep things simple, you could purchase a small amount of ports for this purpose. This allows you the flexibility and ability to setup a video conferencing room for specific purposes without necessarily having to worry about the user having an individual license.

While the above example is one of a very few in which a ports model could work, it in fact would NOT make sense if the users of the “selling room” were also using the webtouch selling presentation tool at their desktop...the assumption being they would already have an individual user account which they could use.

SUMMARY

There are typically only three main pricing models available to you, which helps to keep things simple. You should also be able to mix-and-match as your needs may dictate. In fact some organizations maintain all three, based on situations. Also keep in mind that different models can have different contractual terms. If you need 3 months of a minutes model as you move users to licenses, then ask for it (and see the next chapter)!

Chapter 12 HOW TO ENGAGE WITH THE VENDORS AND FIND THE RIGHT PERSON TO SPEAK WITH

Did you read anything else in this book, or did you immediately flip to this section??? Come on, be honest! Here is where our insider's knowledge will pay for this book hundreds, thousands, or even millions of times over. This chapter in itself will save you huge amounts of time, energy, and money...enjoy!

UNDERSTANDING WHO YOU WILL BE WORKING WITH

It is important to understand the structures of these companies, and the roles of the Account Managers. The easiest way is to describe my role as a Territory Account Manager, and how I am supported. I, as most Account Managers do, handle a geographic territory in which any organization or company whose headquarters are in one of my zip codes belongs to me. The only deviation from this could be if the company is considered an Enterprise account, such as the Walmarts, Boeings, or GEs of the world. Or, if the organization is a government entity or academic institution then they would also fall under the management of a specialist in that area. Otherwise, regardless of anything else, the relationship belongs to me.

The importance in understanding this is that you cannot go around the Account Manager. You will ultimately end up paying what you are able to come to agreement on with this person...no getting a second opinion or getting around it. So make sure you maintain good business relationship skills here. And also keep in mind that Account Manager definitely wants your business, but may be willing to give it up if they feel the working relationship is not worth their time.

Account Managers are usually supported by a front line. These are the folks answering the toll-free hotline, and administering online chats. Their main responsibility is typically to engage in an initial conversation with you, determine the scope of your needs, and get the Account Manager involved if necessary. If the need is for just a handful of individual licenses or less, they will usually accommodate you.

So how does my organization get started?

So by now you have hopefully developed a firm understanding of what the webtouch selling tools are, why they are used, how they can be applied, who offers them, and how they are priced. Now it is time to get the conversations started with the companies themselves, and ultimately make the final purchasing decision.

Talk to your IT department

We suggest this as a first step because the folks in IT are ultimately going to get involved anyway. While they are usually not involved in your organization's sales efforts, they are involved in decisions to purchase technology. If anything, just let them know you are looking at purchasing some webtouch selling software. They could do one of several things:

- Reply, "that's nice"

- Recommend a provider from previous experiences
- Ask to be kept in the loop, especially if your sales team will constantly be broadcasting video, or if your organization needs to worry about things such as HIPAA compliance
- Suggest you reach out to a partner who has supplied them with other technology
- Any of several other responses.

The important thing to know is that the IT department can be your best friend, or your worst enemy. The last thing you want to do is spend a bunch of time finding the webtouch provider you want to work with, only to have your IT department tell you that provider's software or technology is not secure enough.

START MAKING PHONE CALLS

The best way to find who to talk with is to call the providers directly. Find the website or web page for the webtouch selling tools, and call the number provided. They will probably ask you a few questions to determine your initial needs, and how to route your call. If you are looking for a small number of licenses, or know exactly what you need, then the person who answers the phone will probably be able to help you out. However if your needs are deemed to be a bit more complex, or if that phone rep has decided that your account needs go beyond just an individual license or two, then they will forward your information to the Territory Account Manager who is responsible for the relationship with your company.

Online Chat

Most providers also offer an online chat feature which can be accessed directly from their website. Again, visit the website and find a chat icon to be immediately be connected with a live representative. This will function the same way as making a phone call in the sense that they will qualify you appropriately, and either help you or forward you to the Account Manager.

Website Request

This is an easy and straightforward way to be connected to the appropriate Account Manager. As long as you fill in your correct contact information, expect a call or email within a couple of days.

Download a free trial

Another way to easily get engaged with the appropriate Account Manager is to simply download a free trial of the software itself. If you already know that you just need a small handful of licenses, this is a great way to go. You should already understand that the probable pricing model will be the individual license one, and simply need to do a test-drive. Your information will automatically be directed to the appropriate person on the provider end, assuming you put in the correct zip code. The Account Manager will receive a daily report indicating free-trial downloads in their territory, and contact you directly. Please note that if you do NOT put in correct information, it can lead to misrouting, and/or speaking with the wrong Account Manager. If this happens, you will ultimately be forwarded to the right one, and your discussions will probably start all over.

Free trials are a great way to get started, and probably the most commonly used way. But most of the providers only offer free trials of one of the webtouch selling applications. For example, at the present time CISCO only allows you to run a free trial of their online presentation tool. They do not offer this for the webinar, training, or support tool. You can, by the way get free evaluation accounts of these tools, but only at the discretion of the Account Manager (more on negotiating these fully functional evaluation versions later).

So the point here is that you do not need to take on this task alone, and utilize the knowledge of the Account Manager. At their levels they are not trained simply to product push. They will usually schedule at least an hour or so to speak with you, and fully understand what you are looking to accomplish. They will probably speak with you about the entire webtouch selling process, and help determine where you are, and where you want to be. Once this is done, then, and only then, will product recommendations be made. My suggestion would be to move on if you are not impressed with their expertise. But hopefully this book has armed you with enough knowledge to help them help you!

Working with a partner

As discussed earlier, working through a partner can be a very wise choice when acquiring your webtouch selling software. Usually, if your organization has more than 100 or so employees, there will be an existing relationship with a local, regional, or national reseller of IT products and services. The absolute best way to find this out is to ask your IT department. If you are looking at more than around 25 users, the partner can be a great resource as they can usually offer these quantities through pre-negotiated prices that you cannot get by going direct. If you are under the 25 license realm, then you will probably not go the partner route, unless insisted upon by your IT department.

Working with a Service Provider

Along the same lines of working with a Certified Partner, working with a Service Provider will usually be done in larger organizations where the relationship already exists. Again, check with your IT or telecom department to see if this could be an option. And just as working with a Certified Partner, just because it is possible does not mean it is the best idea. Use what you have learned throughout this book to make the right decision.

Summary

Finding the right person to speak with should be easy.

But remember...this person is ultimately responsible for the relationship with your organization, and prices that you will pay.

There is always room for discounts, reduced terms, free evaluations, and other goodies. Try to maintain a good working relationship with this person. The better the relationship between you both, the easier the process will be, and the higher the likelihood that you will have easy and successful negations. Now read on for the best part of our insider's information!

Chapter 13 The Money Chapter – Negotiating the Contract, with a Little More Help from the Inside!

So everything boils down to money doesn't it? Let's face it...you're reading this book so that you can increase sales and make more of it! And the better the pricing you get on your purchase of webtouch selling software the better your ROI will be. So let's talk about what can and can't be negotiated, who has control of what, good times to buy, and set some realistic expectations. And PLEASE keep this thought at the front of your mind..."If you don't ask for it, then the answer is always NO!"

WHO SETS THE PRICING?

Every single provider of webtouch selling software has what is called "list price". These are the prices set by an individual or group located behind the curtain in the wonderful Land of Oz. They are called list prices only because they appear on the Account Manager's list, which probably hangs on their office wall, or is bookmarked in their web browser. The final price will be set by the Account Manager, and is a result of negotiations. Keep in mind that a lot of times list pricing WILL have to be paid, but these times are rare.

When will we pay list price?

For the most part, this is straightforward enough and there is a rule-of-thumb. If the price is listed on the website, you will probably pay it, regardless of who you speak with. For example, if you go to the WebEx website, you will see that the beginning package starts at $49 per month for an individual license of their corporate product Meeting Center Pro. You can sign up online, but only for a maximum of 9 licenses. These licenses would be for $49 apiece. If you called the Account Manager, you would still pay the $49 per license.

The idea behind the number 9 is that CISCO feels that if your organization needs more than this, then you have advanced needs. Don't shun away from this. Advanced needs means advanced pricing, and advanced discounts! I have seen scenarios where purchasing 12 licenses ended up being less expensive than purchasing 9 through the website!

Pricing the other tools

The other webtouch selling tools (webinar, training, support, and EIM) are all considered more advanced tools than the online presentation one. This is because they have different features and functionality which are tailored more to their business group or end users. These applications are also more expensive than the online presentation tool (except for the EIM tool, which is usually at the MOST a couple bucks per user per month). It is rare that you will be able to purchase any of these tools directly from the provider's website. But this is good, because that means the prices are negotiable!

Price is negotiable

To begin, the costs per license, minute, or port are all negotiable when talking about volume. Instead of looking at individual prices of specific products, we're going to make this real easy. The maximum discounts you can typically receive when working directly with a webtouch selling software provider are 40%. However the AVERAGE is about 20%. Why the difference?

Account Managers have a threshold which they can approve without seeking approval from the Wizard. That threshold is typically 20% off of the list pricing. In order for them to go higher, they need to seek approvals and must be armed with a good business case. This is where you can truly help yourself by maintaining open communications with the Account Manager and at least have them believe in your cause, and that you won't go away or not pay your bills. It is ALWAYS a good idea to ask what list price is, just as you would ask a car dealership what the sticker price is. Expect your final price to be around 20% off list, and try for 40%!

Terms are Negotiable

The terms of your contract are usually finalized with an initial term, and then the renewal term. For example, a 12/12 would have an initial term of 12 months, and then renew on the anniversary date for another 12 months (also known as an annual agreement). Most companies will even offer a discount if the 12 months are paid for up front.

But signing an annual contract may not be the best idea for your situation or organization. What if you are in the beginning stages of setting up a webtouch selling model, and don't know if it will fully kick in as you have planned? Or maybe you have an approved budget, and that budget will be re-assessed after 6 months if your plan is working. Here is where you can negotiate for a better initial term. For example, a 6/12 would mean that your initial term would be for 6 months, and then it would renew for 12.

It is very important to note that term reductions don't just come easily. Chances are high that your Account Manager has been paid for the full year. If you cancel your agreement after 6 months, they get docked the remaining 6 months. You are certain to have to give something in return for the reduced term. Usually it is found in the price. They can never go above list, but they can give you 10% off instead of 20%!

Terms from the website are usually month-to-month by default, with a discount given for annual prepay. This is purposefully done in order to get new users, with the ultimate goal of upgrading you to more licenses, services, and longer terms. The chances of you securing a month-to-month term on any offer other than what is on the website are very slim. But it has been done!

Evaluation Accounts

As mentioned earlier, fully functioning evaluation accounts are available from your Account Manager. These are similar to the free trials, but different in the sense that your AM should be able to set you up with an evaluation account for ANY of their offered webtouch selling tools, and the account usually won't automatically expire.

A good working relationship with your AM is the best way to secure an evaluation account. There is some work that goes into setting up the account, as well as a fear that someone will use it to conduct a "free" webinar! You are also very likely to effectively request evaluation accounts if you are talking about purchasing multiple licenses. Be prepared to give a little back to the Account Manager in exchange for the evaluation accounts. This could come in the form of tracking down user information, or providing dates for having your purchasing decisions made.

Free Months of Service

A free month is another tool the Account Manager will typically have in his arsenal in order to entice you to purchase their webtouch selling software instead of a competitor's. But again, you may have to give something up in return for this. Usually it is not increased pricing, but a longer term. When the AM gives you a free month, they don't get paid for that month. Adding a sense of security that you will not leave before 12 months is good reason for them to offer you this. And if you do sign a 12 month agreement, make sure and ask for the free month!

Other goodies, freebies, and incentives

The major companies will sometimes have other things sitting around the office which they can use to gain your business. Probably the most common thing you can find is a webcam. If you are looking at purchasing 25 or more licenses, ask for a half-dozen webcams. They are in fact happy to give you these as they can lead to a better adoption of their webtouch selling software.

Negotiating through a partner

If you are using a partner to purchase the webtouch selling software for you, negotiating is a bit more straightforward. Your partner will typically be purchasing the software for between 42% and 50% off of the list price, and then add their markup on top of that. The list price provided to partners is usually different than the list pricing provided when going direct, but should be pretty close. Whether they are willing to discuss their pricing with you or not is really up to them. But you can usually count on them marking it up anywhere from 8-15%...they have to make money too. Keep in mind that terms are usually NOT negotiable through a partner, as the offerings they have access to are typically 1 – 5 years of service, with discounts given for longer term commitments.

NEGOTIATING THROUGH A SERVICE PROVIDER

This one can be tricky, as there can be a lot of moving parts. If you are planning on purchasing your webtouch selling software through a Service Provider, then it is important to speak with your IT and/or telecom department in order to figure out what else you may already be purchasing from them.

Perhaps the BEST thing you can negotiate through a Service Provider is uncommitted pricing. Now at the time of this being written, uncommitted business is a hot topic. The main reason is this...the Account Managers at the Service Providers are compensated differently than just about everyone else. They typically get paid on your actual usage, instead of committed usage. And if you go on an uncommitted plan, the Account Manager who works for the Direct Provider does not get compensated at all! While uncommitted can be a good thing because of its flexibility, you should expect to pay higher prices than if you made a commitment, and receive little to no support from the Direct Provider.

A MUST to remember is that if you ARE committed, then everyone else is too...committed to your success, and effective use of their software and services.

Another thing to note about working through a Service Provider is that they can usually offer you web conferencing tools of their own. These are proprietary services directly from them, and not one of the major Direct Provider's software. While sometimes less expensive, they usually lack in many features. Additionally, the Account Managers at Service Providers can sometimes be compensated more by selling their proprietary webtouch tools. Again, the cost savings can outweigh the features, but make sure you fully understand what you are getting.

SOME TIMES ARE BETTER THAN OTHERS TO PURCHASE ENTERPRISE SOFTWARE

The major companies that offer webtouch selling software are all publicly traded. This means that they report their numbers to Wall Street at the end of each of their fiscal quarters, and at the end of every fiscal year. Account Managers are much more likely to fight for higher discounts towards the end of these quarters, especially if they have not yet hit their quotas.

When you have chosen which vendor you want to partner with, find their fiscal calendar! And unless you have an extreme pressing need, then you should wait until the end of their fiscal quarter is approaching before making your purchase. You may find that you can get 40% off, reduced terms, a free month, AND free webcams! Also keep this in the very forefront of your mind...if you come through for an Account Manager and sign a contract for them at the end of their fiscal quarter, they will probably become your BEST friend! I cannot stress enough how valuable this can be for the duration of your relationship with them. Trust me...scratch their back, and they will scratch yours!

SUMMARY

The goal of this chapter was to give you a better understanding of how webtouch selling software is priced, what can be negotiated, how to do it, and when to do it. But at the end of the day, the most important decision you can make for your sales efforts is to make the purchase, and implement a webtouch selling model!

Chapter 14 Conclusion and Action Items

Hopefully your reading of this book has led you to the understanding of how effective webtouch selling tools can be for your organization. Sales revenue is the lifeblood of any organization, and these applications have been purposefully built to help bring in the money. There is never a "bad" time to implement a webtouch selling model, and the sooner you do it the faster your sales will increase. And we all have a saying in our industry..."No one has ever been fired for choosing to use these tools!"

The last chapters in this book should have laid out the processes in which to determine which of the webtouch selling tools you need, who to purchase them from, and how to negotiate and acquire them. There are, however some steps you will also want to go through internally in order to make sure you have buy-in from all of the stakeholders. Make sure you cover the following bases in order to make the migration to a webtouch selling sales model as smooth as possible:

- Have internal discussions with each of the departments who will be using the webtouch selling tools. These include sales and marketing, training, support, and general operations.
- Meet with the IT department so that they can be in the loop, and provide guidance if needed.
- Set expectations for results, and attach timelines to them. While a webtouch selling model should gain immediate traction and be easily maintained, it may turn out that your organization is simply not ready. Having a "retreat plan" in place will set other stakeholders at ease.

Take your game to the next level, and use these tools to skyrocket your revenue. Happy Selling!!!

ABOUT THE AUTHOR

T. B. Hodge lives in Jacksonville, Florida with his wonderful family of four. A North Carolina native, T. B. found his way to Jacksonville via Tallahassee, FL where he received a degree in Economics from Florida State University. He has a passion for selling, as well as a passion for teaching, both of which led to his authoring of Webtouch Selling. He hopes you enjoy the book, use the knowledge effectively, and have it be a direct influence on more sales for your organization.

www.ingramcontent.com/pod-product-compliance
Lightning Source LLC
Chambersburg PA
CBHW071841200326
41519CB00016B/4190

* 9 7 8 0 9 8 5 2 4 9 9 1 5 *